first 5

first 15

© First15

No part of this publication may be reproduced, distributed or transmitted in any form or by any means, including photocopying or electronic or mechanical method without prior written permission of the editor; except in the case of brief quotations embodied in critical reviews and certain other noncommercial uses permitted by copyright law. For permissions request, please write to us.

"Scripture quotations are from The ESV® Bible (The Holy Bible, English Standard Version®), copyright © 2001 by Crossway, a publishing ministry of Good News Publishers. Used by permission. All rights reserved."

Printed in Dallas, Texas by The Odee Company

Contact: contact@first15.org
www.first15.org

Layout Designed by Matt Ravenelle
mattravenelle.com

Images curated from
Unsplash

ABOUT FIRST15

Spending time alone with God every day can be a struggle. We're busier – and more stressed – than ever. But still, we know it's important to spend time alone with our Creator. We know we need to read his word, pray, and worship him.

First15 bridges the gap between desire and reality, helping you establish the rhythm of meaningful, daily experiences in God's presence. First15 answers the critical questions:

- Why should I spend time alone with God?
- How do I spend time alone with God?
- How do I get the most out of my time alone with God?
- How can I become more consistent with my time alone with God?

And by answering these questions through the format of daily devotionals, you'll practice the rhythm of meeting with God while experiencing the incredible gift of his loving presence given to those who make time to meet with him.

Allow God's passionate pursuit to draw you in across the next several days. And watch as every day is better than the last as your life is built on the solid foundation of God's love through the power of consistent, meaningful time alone with him.

To learn more about First15, visit our website first15.org. First15 is available across mobile app, email, podcast, and our website. Subscribe to our devotional today and experience God in a fresh way every day.

ABOUT THE AUTHOR

Craig Denison is the author of First15, a daily devotional guiding over a million believers into a fresh experience with God every day. In 2015, Craig founded First15 after sensing a longing in God's heart for his people to be about relationship – real, restored relationship with him – that above all else, he simply wanted the hearts of his people. Craig began praying, dreaming, and writing. And the idea of helping people spend the first fifteen minutes of their day focusing on nothing else but growing in their relationship with God was born. The vision was birthed in Craig's heart that if we as a people would worship, read, and pray at the beginning of every day, everything could change for the better. Craig writes, speaks, and he and his wife, Rachel lead worship to help believers establish a more tangible, meaningful connection with God.

CONTENTS

Tiling the soil of your heart
Week 1

The desires of every heart
Week 2

Parables
Week 3

Vision and boundaries
Week 4

Day 1	Tilling the Soil of the Heart	12-15
Day 2	Tilling the Soil of the Heart: Thankfulness	16-19
Day 3	Tilling the Soil of the Heart: Worship	20-23
Day 4	Tilling the Soil of the Heart: Scripture	24-27
Day 5	Tilling the Soil of the Heart: The Body of Christ	28-31
Day 6	Tilling the Soil of the Heart: Prayer	32-35
Day 7	Tilling the Soil of the Heart: God's Voice	36-39
Day 8	The Desire to be Delighted in	46-49
Day 9	The Desire for Wonder	50-53
Day 10	The Desire to Behold Beauty	54-57
Day 11	The Desire to be Great	58-61
Day 12	The Desire to be Fully Known and Fully Loved	62-65
Day 13	The Desire to be Passionate	66-69
Day 14	The Desire to Live a Life of Significance	70-73
Day 15	The Parable of the Good Shepherd	80-83
Day 16	The Parables of the Hidden Treasure and Valuable Pearl	84-87
Day 17	The Parable of the Mustard Seed	88-91
Day 18	The Parable of the Lamp on a Stand	92-95
Day 19	The Parable of the Pharisee and the Tax Collector	96-99
Day 20	The Parable of the Prodigal Son	100-103
Day 21	The Parables of the Lost Sheep and Coin	104-107
Day 22	Being a Person of Vision	114-117
Day 23	Vision for God	118-120
Day 24	Vision for Yourself	122-125
Day 25	Vision for Others	126-129
Day 26	Vision for Work	130-133
Day 27	Vision for Community	134-137
Day 28	Vision for Eternity	138-141

DAYS 1 - 7

Tiling the soil of your heart

01

WEEK

"As for that in the good soil, they are those who, hearing the word, hold it fast in an honest and good heart, and bear fruit with patience." Luke 8:15

WEEKLY OVERVIEW

This week we'll look at a vital spiritual practice to all those seeking to grow in God: tilling the soil of the heart. Jesus spoke in Matthew 13 of two different types of soil—hard and soft. God longs for us to till the soil of our hearts that we might be receptive to the seed of his word and bear fruit. May your heart become more responsive to the presence, will, and love of God this week as you cultivate good soil with the help of the Holy Spirit.

Tilling the Soil of the Heart

DAY 1

DEVOTIONAL

Matthew 13:22-23 says, *"As for what was sown among thorns, this is the one who hears the word, but the cares of the world and the deceitfulness of riches choke the word, and it proves unfruitful. As for what was sown on good soil, this is the one who hears the word and understands it. He indeed bears fruit and yields, in one case a hundredfold, in another sixty, and in another thirty."*

"As for what was sown on good soil, this is the one who hears the word and understands it. He indeed bears fruit and yields, in one case a hundredfold, in another sixty, and in another thirty."

MATTHEW 13:23

The concept of good and bad soil is something Jesus's listeners would have understood well. Planting in good or bad soil meant having food or going hungry. It meant having money or not. For their agrarian culture it was a matter of survival.

While Jesus's parable might not have as direct a correlation to us, its principle remains just as relevant. We all have spiritual soil. Through our mindsets and postures of the heart we can receive the seed of God's word which will in turn yield life-giving fruit. Or, we can allow the soil of our hearts to make us unreceptive to the powerful work God in our lives.

It's incredibly important for us to understand that God never forces his desires on us. He waits patiently—beckoning us to open our hearts fully to him. He gently shows us his love, whispers his perfect plans to us, and waits for us to trust and surrender. With the grace of God, we can till the soil of our hearts, living receptively and surrendered to his loving kindness and perfect will. If we will cultivate a willing heart, God will mold and shape us into children free from the cares of the world and empowered to live Christ-like, fruitful lives.

Take time today to assess your own life. What parts of your heart are hard to God? Where do you feel unreceptive to his goodness? Where do you need to say yes to God today in a fresh, transformative way? God is calling you to a lifestyle of trust and surrender that he might lead you to green pastures and still waters. There is abundant life for you in store this week as you cultivate good soil. May the Holy Spirit help you look honestly at the posture of your heart today as you enter into a time of guided prayer.

GUIDED PRAYER

1. Take some time to receive God's presence. Open your heart to feel the peace and rest that comes from encountering him.

"My presence will go with you, and I will give you rest." Exodus 33:14

2. Ask the Holy Spirit to reveal to you ways in which you aren't fully open to God. How are you not fully saying yes to God? In what ways are you living your life apart from the leadership and presence of God? Where don't you fully trust him? Where aren't you bearing the fruit of the Spirit?

"But the fruit of the Spirit is love, joy, peace, patience, kindness, goodness, faithfulness, gentleness, self-control; against such things there is no law." Galatians 5:22-23

3. Confess those things to God. Receive his love and forgiveness as you repent and turn away from hardness of heart. Spend time resting in God's presence and experiencing the new found peace that comes from having your heart more surrendered and receptive to God.

"If we confess our sins, he is faithful and just to forgive us our sins and to cleanse us from all unrighteousness." 1 John 1:9

Tilling our hearts into good soil is an important daily exercise. The more often you do it, the more you'll realize the need to have good soil. Having our hearts fully open to God takes the mundane and makes it wonderful. It takes sunsets, conversations, prayers, work, and church and fills them with life, value, beauty, and joy. Take what you've learned today and continue to put it into practice. Choose to live a life positioned to receive all that God has in store for you. May your day be marked by the fruit of the Spirit.

Extended Reading: Matthew 13

WEEK 1

Tilling the Soil of the Heart: Thankfulness

DAY 2

DEVOTIONAL

Thankfulness is one of the most powerful tools in making our hearts both soft to the seed of God's word and filled with abundant joy. Thanksgiving aligns our thoughts and emotions with the reality of God's goodness in a world wrought with lies about the character of God. It breeds joy and trust rather than entitlement and negativity. With each declaration of thankfulness you dig a shovel into the hard, rocky soil of your heart and churn it over until it becomes receptive to the fullness of God and filled with the fruit of the Spirit.

*"Oh give thanks to the Lord, for he is good,
for his steadfast love endures forever!"*

PSALM 107:1

The Bible is laden with commands to be thankful. Ephesians 5:20 tells us to be *"giving thanks always and for everything to God the Father in the name of our Lord Jesus Christ."* Philippians 4:6 tells us, *"Do not be anxious about anything, but in everything by prayer and supplication with thanksgiving let your requests be made known to God."* But my favorite command on thankfulness is Psalm 107:1, *"Oh give thanks to the Lord, for he is good, for his steadfast love endures forever!"*

You see, it's important to understand that the Bible doesn't suggest that we give thanks, but rather commands us to always be thankful. And in God's command he reveals his heart. We learn in Psalm 107 that our thankfulness is meant to be a response to the steadfast love of our heavenly Father. Thankfulness is meant to be the overflow of remembering, encountering and mulling over how our God is abundantly faithful and filled with unconditional love for us.

I used to read Scripture commanding me to be thankful and think, "Sorry God, I know I need to be more thankful. I know I'm so provided for and loved. I'm sorry for not thanking you more." But after meditating on Psalm 107:1, I realized that my lack of thankfulness is a symptom of not spending enough time encountering God's wonderful character rather than a core issue in and of itself. Tilling the soil of my heart through thankfulness requires that I set aside time to simply experience God's goodness and love. Because everything he does is by grace, my natural response to his character will always be one of thanksgiving.

Take time today to reflect on the faithful and loving character of your heavenly Father. Allow his goodness to cause thankfulness to well up within you. May your time in guided prayer be filled with a transformational encounter with God and cultivate good soil that bears the fruit of an abundant life.

GUIDED PRAYER

1. Reflect on the faithful and loving character of your heavenly Father.

"Have you not known? Have you not heard? The Lord is the everlasting God, the Creator of the ends of the earth. He does not faint or grow weary; his understanding is unsearchable." Isaiah 40:28

"This God—his way is perfect; the word of the Lord proves true; he is a shield for all those who take refuge in him." Psalm 18:30

"Bless the Lord, O my soul, and all that is within me, bless his holy name! Bless the Lord, O my soul, and forget not all his benefits, who forgives all your iniquity, who heals all your diseases, who redeems your life from the pit, who crowns you with steadfast love and mercy, who satisfies you with good so that your youth is renewed like the eagle's." Psalm 103:1-5

2. Now respond to God's character with thankfulness. Take Scripture and thank God for who he is. Look at your life and thank God for any good gifts he's given you. Allow his goodness to stir up thankfulness within you.

"Oh give thanks to the Lord, for he is good, for his steadfast love endures forever!" Psalm 107:1

3. What changed in your heart as you engaged in thanksgiving? Journal about the power of thankfulness. Ask the Holy Spirit to help you see how God is at work in your life today and offer thanksgiving in response.

If you start to feel your heart begin to harden because of something that happens today, simply reflect on the goodness of God and give thanks. Negativity and sin have an incredibly harmful effect on our hearts. Decide to put away any form of slander, impurity and anything negative at all, and instead focus on the goodness of what God is doing. Choose to love today and align your thoughts and emotions with faith and trust in who God is. To walk in relationship with God is to follow the leading of the Holy Spirit at all times. If you get off track for a bit, simply ask the Spirit to lead you back to the perspective and posture of heart he desires for you! God's grace is abounding and powerful. He longs to walk in relationship with you all day today. May your day be filled with peace, joy and a passionate pursuit of bringing his kingdom to earth all around you.

Extended Reading: 1 Thessalonians 5:12-28

Tilling the Soil of the Heart: Worship

DAY 3

DEVOTIONAL

One of the most powerful ways to till the soil of the heart is through worship. Authentic worship is a powerful exchange of God pouring his love out on us and us giving him our hearts in return. In worshiping through music, our hearts naturally become soft and receptive to God's love as we encounter his goodness and engage in adoration of the only One worthy of our affections.

WEEK 1

*"Ascribe to the Lord the glory due his name;
worship the Lord in the splendor of holiness."*

PSALM 29:2

God created music with an innate ability to affect us at our core. Music has the power to fill us with peace, joy, and anger; it can cause tears to well up in our eyes and even make the most mundane events beautiful. Martin Luther said, "Beautiful music is the art of the prophets that can calm the agitations of the soul; it is one of the most magnificent and delightful presents God has given us." By consistently engaging in worship through beautiful music, we provide a framework for the Holy Spirit both to till the soil of our hearts and to fill us with the seeds of God's presence and perfect character.

The Bible is brimming with admonishment to worship through song. Paul tells us in Colossians 3:16, *"Let the word of Christ dwell in you richly, teaching and admonishing one another in all wisdom, singing psalms and hymns and spiritual songs, with thankfulness in your hearts to God."* Hebrews 12:28 says, *"Therefore let us be grateful for receiving a kingdom that cannot be shaken, and thus let us offer to God acceptable worship, with reverence and awe."* Scripture is so clear about the importance of worship because God longs for us to be a people marked by consistent reminders of his unconditional love. He longs for us to live in response to his presence and plans rather than struggling through life by placing our trust in the world over him.

God longs to reveal his heart to you in worship. He longs to show up and meet you in your room, car, workplace, and house of worship. You were created to encounter God and engage in the cyclical act of giving and receiving love throughout your day. When you worship here on earth, you posture your heart towards eternity. Making the willful choice to give your affections to the One you will spend eternity with, you also discover your purpose for which you were made: to live in unhindered communion with your heavenly Father.

If you feel like the soil of your heart is hard, your life isn't marked by the fruit of the Spirit or you can't escape from a temptation—simply take some time and encounter God in worship. God's presence is wholly available to you today. His love and grace are steadfast towards you. May your time in guided prayer be marked by the nearness and power of the Holy Spirit as you encounter the unconditional love of God.

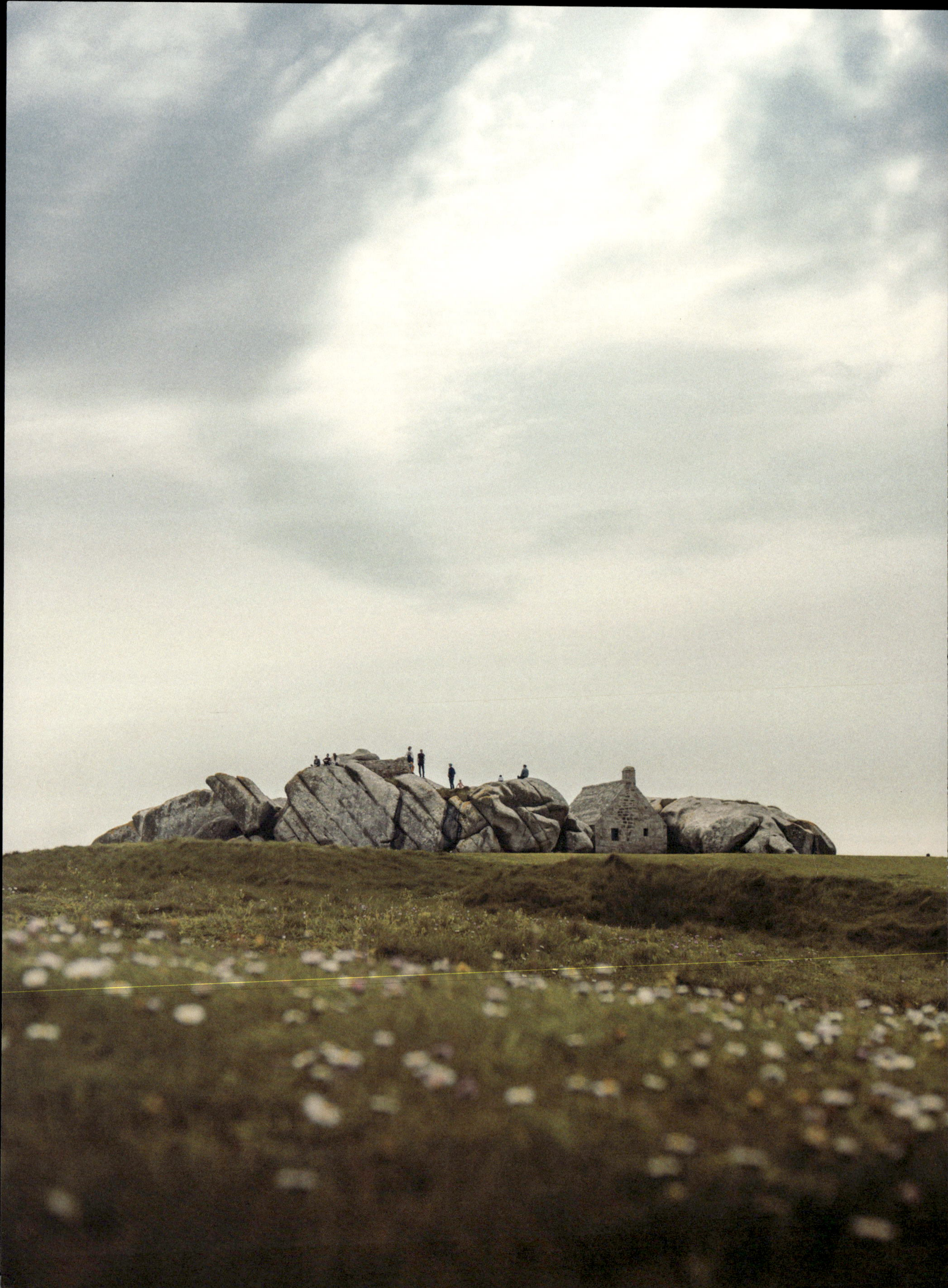

GUIDED PRAYER

1. Meditate on what Scripture says about worship through music and reflect on how beautiful music moves your heart.

"Make a joyful noise to the Lord, all the earth! Serve the Lord with gladness! Come into his presence with singing! Know that the Lord, he is God! It is he who made us, and we are his; we are his people, and the sheep of his pasture. Enter his gates with thanksgiving, and his courts with praise! Give thanks to him; bless his name! For the Lord is good; his steadfast love endures forever, and his faithfulness to all generations." Psalm 100:1-5

"And whenever the harmful spirit from God was upon Saul, David took the lyre and played it with his hand. So Saul was refreshed and was well, and the harmful spirit departed from him." 1 Samuel 16:23

2. Engage in worship in whatever way moves your heart. Receive the presence and love of your heavenly Father and give him your heart in response. Remember the importance of giving and receiving love in worship.

"My heart is steadfast, O God, my heart is steadfast! I will sing and make melody!" Psalm 57:7

"I will sing to the Lord, because he has dealt bountifully with me." Psalm 13:6

3. Journal about the effects worship has on your heart. Reflecting on and writing down the things God is doing in our lives helps us to actualize that which is often left internal and forgotten.

Psalm 104:33 says, *"I will sing to the Lord as long as I live; I will sing praise to my God while I have being."* Until your life is devoted to worshipping God, you will never find total rest. When we give ourselves to the things of this world it repays us with stress, burden, and cares rather than unconditional love. It's only in devoting yourself to God alone that you will find satisfaction and reciprocation for your love. Live today in full devotion to God. Do everything as an act of worship. And find that God repays your adoration ten fold by pouring out his wealth of affection over you. May today be filled with the presence and power of God as you give and receive love.

Extended Reading: Ephesians 5:1-21

Tilling the Soil of the Heart: Scripture

DAY 4

DEVOTIONAL

One of the most powerful tools in tilling the soil of our hearts is Scripture. Each time you open the Bible you're looking at a miracle. 2 Timothy 3:16 tells us, *"All Scripture is breathed out by God and profitable for teaching, for reproof, for correction, and for training in righteousness."* When you are reading the Bible, you are reading the very word of God, breathed out by him and powerful in its ability to

> *"Blessed is the man who walks not in the counsel of the wicked, nor stands in the way of sinners, nor sits in the seat of scoffers; but his delight is in the law of the Lord, and on his law he meditates day and night."*

PSALM 1:1-2

reveal both the character of God and your identity. Romans 12:2 says, *"Do not be conformed to this world, but be transformed by the renewal of your mind."* When you renew your mind through Scripture, you allow the Bible to transform your heart into fertile soil that bears everlasting fruit. So let's look today at a few ways we can use Scripture to renew our minds and allow it to mold and shape us into disciples who are in tune with and receptive to the love and leading of God.

There is a wealth of power and wisdom within God's word as it reveals his love and faithfulness to his people. Stories of God's deliverance and provision to an ungrateful people demonstrate not only God's faithfulness then, but also the great lengths he will go to for those ransomed into his family now by the blood of Christ. The story of Jesus' sacrifice for our sins is both heart wrenching and life giving. That he would willingly endure one of the most heinous, tortuous methods ever created assures us of the love God has for us. That he would experience separation from his heavenly Father for the sin of the entire world points to the depth of his love for us. Reading stories like these and meditating on their meaning and application will make us receptive to the presence and will of God. They can empower us to live in grateful obedience to his plans and purposes.

As Paul wrote in Second Timothy, the Bible is also a useful tool for life-giving correction. Correction from God is an important and wonderful part of being his son or daughter. His correction resembles a skilled gardener pulling the weeds out of soil, making room for seeds he has planted to receive nourishment and thereby flourish into fruit. You see, God doesn't correct out of anger or frustration, but rather out of his rich love, patience, and desire for us to walk in the abundant life he's prepared for us. Proverbs 3:12 states, *"The Lord reproves him whom he loves, as a father the son in whom he delights."* So, opening our hearts to Scripture like Ephesians 4:29, *"Let no corrupting talk come out of your mouths, but only such as is good for building up, as fits the occasion, that it may give grace to those who hear,"* is incredibly powerful. Pulling out the weeds of corrupting or negative talk will create space in the soil of our hearts for the nourishment of God's Spirit, yielding the fruit of speech that does indeed *"give grace."*

Open your heart today to the power of God's word in tilling the soil of your heart. Allow the Holy Spirit to teach you by speaking directly into your life using the words of Scripture. May your time in guided prayer be marked by the inner voice of the Spirit and transformation of the heart.

GUIDED PRAYER

1. Ask the Spirit to reveal an area in which you need correction. Think about something in your life that is hurting your ability to develop good soil and thereby good fruit. Where are you not experiencing the abundant life Jesus died to give you?

"I came that they may have life and have it abundantly."
John 10:10

2. Now search for Scripture to use for meditation on the subject. If you feel that negative speech is hindering you, a verse like Ephesians 4:29 that we read earlier is a great start. If you feel like lust or another sin is hindering you, search for Scriptures addressing the sin you struggle with.

3. Meditate on the Scripture that you've found. Allow God to apply Scripture directly to your life.

When we align ourselves with God's word, we lose the burden of living life apart from the anointing and filling of his Spirit. Giving up things like negative speech, lust, greed, and other sins creates space for that which brings life and abundance. Today, give over anything you feel is crowding your spiritual life, and allow God to fill you with the grace to live according to his word. His word is the perfect guide through every situation, useful for any occasion. Allow the Spirit to speak to you both through the Bible and directly. Till the soil of your heart to be receptive to all that he would do in and through you today.

Extended Reading: 2 Kings 22-23

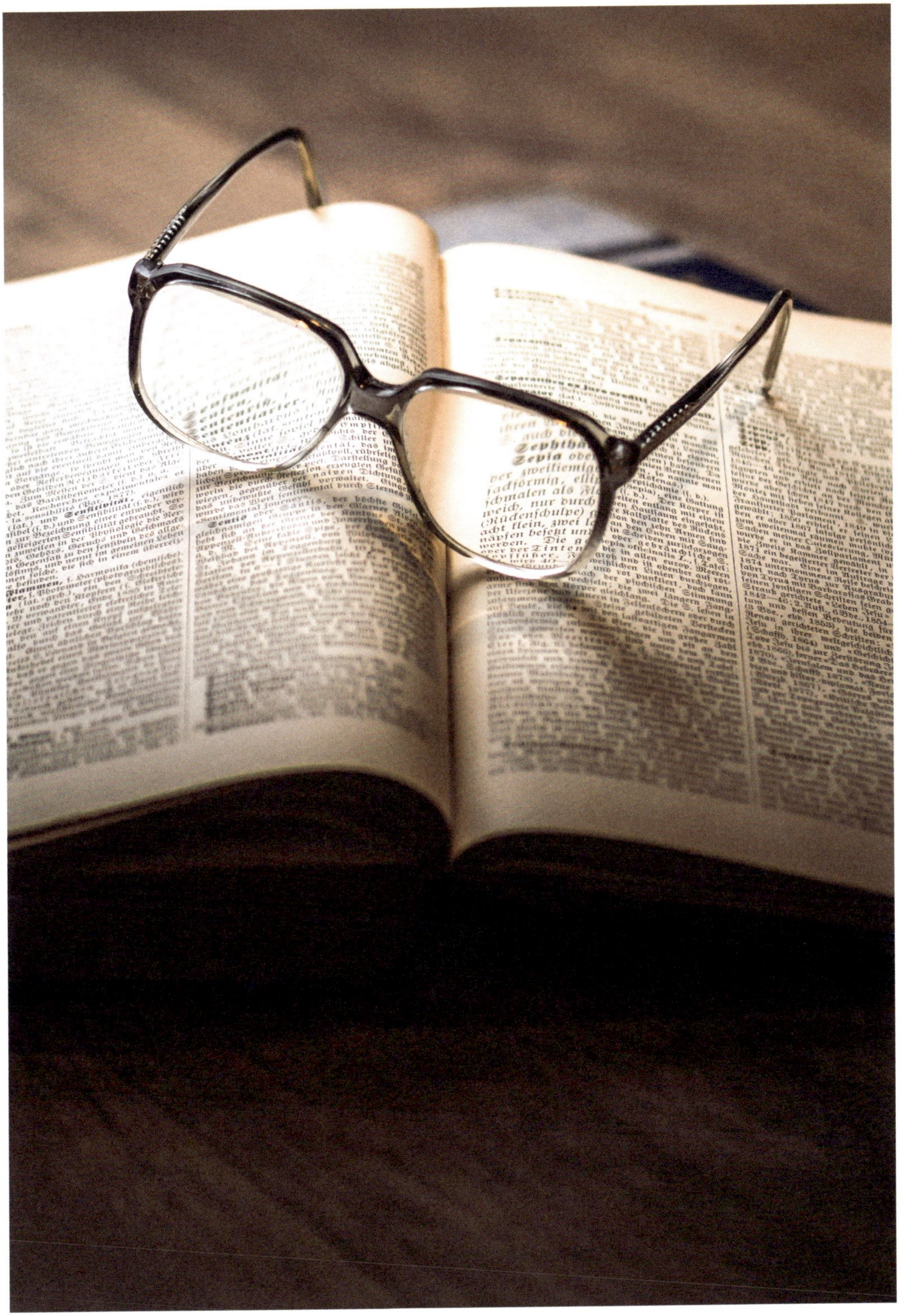

Tilling the Soil of the Heart: The Body of Christ

DAY 5

DEVOTIONAL

One of the most useful gifts God has given us for making our hearts receptive to him is each other. The church is both a beautiful and broken group of people. Beautiful because of the grace of God working in each of us making us more like Jesus. Broken because we have yet to walk in the fullness of what Christ did for us on the cross. Most of us have been wounded by something that happened in a church. Most of us have felt anger, frustration, or annoyance with a fellow believer. But if we are to walk in the fullness of what God intends for us here on earth, we must continually forgive and ask forgiveness from each other, submit ourselves to a group of Christ followers, and share life with believers in accordance with God's word.

The Bible is clear that the best place for us to thrive is in community with fellow believers. Romans 12:5 teaches us that we are all *"one body in Christ, and individually members of one another."* Hebrews 10:24-

*"For as in one body we have many members,
and the members do not all have the same function,
so we, though many, are one body in Christ, and
individually members one of another."*

ROMANS 12:4-5

25 says, *"And let us consider how to stir up one another to love and good works, not neglecting to meet together, as is the habit of some, but encouraging one another, and all the more as you see the Day drawing near."* And Ephesians 4:15-16 teaches us that *"speaking the truth in love, we are to grow up in every way into him who is the head, into Christ, from whom the whole body, joined and held together by every joint with which it is equipped, when each part is working properly, makes the body grow so that it builds itself up in love."* We need each other. We're joined together as the body of Christ made to function as one—both for our edification and the fulfillment of God's eternal purposes in the world.

In order to make the soil of your heart soft and receptive to God, you must have help from those God has placed around you. We are created to worship with the body of Christ for all eternity, and that includes right now! Don't wait to live out the promises of God. The church is not perfect, but it is God's Bride. His desire is for his people, and he loves to pour out his presence in unique and specific ways when we gather together. There is edification you need that can only take place in the presence of fellow believers. There is blessing that can only be received when you open your heart to the family of God. We all have wounds; we all need grace; we all need each other. The very person who most annoys you might need you the most. Just as you need what fellow believers around you have to offer you, others need who God has uniquely designed you to be.

God asks us to humble ourselves before him and each other. Philippians 2:3 teaches us to *"do nothing from selfish ambition or conceit, but in humility count others more significant than yourselves."* When you humble yourself, you will find a peace that is never available in living for your own ambitions. When you submit yourself to imperfect people, you give away your sense of entitlement and find the grace of God that's poured out on those who truly count others as more significant than themselves. It's in the submission to others and giving away of our own rights that the soil of our heart is made soft and receptive to God. It's in spending time with fellow imperfect people that we become edified and are spurred on toward spending more time with God.

Often it's in the extending of grace and forgiveness to each other that we become most like Christ, the one who suffered and died in the ultimate act of humility to we who are unworthy. Offer love to those who don't deserve it. Place yourself in community with those who are imperfect. Open your heart to those who might not treat you with perfect kindness. Find your unique place in the body and serve the community God has placed you in with faithfulness so that you might be fashioned in the likeness of Christ.

GUIDED PRAYER

1. Ask God to show you the community he would have you be a part of. Whether this answer comes immediately or through seeking and visiting churches, trust that God will guide you to the local body he has planned for you.

2. Ask God to show you your place in the community. This will change over time, so it's good to continually ask God this question, especially if you feel out of place.

3. Now ask God to show you how he feels about the church. We aren't meant to live and love out of our own strength. Instead, we are to seek God's heart for his people and align ourselves with him.

God's desire for the church is vast and powerful. He has loved his people in perfect faithfulness despite all our transgressions and wandering. When we fail to show grace and love to those around us, we fail to live out of God's heart for his people. If you want to live a life as near to God's heart as possible you must search him out with the rest of his body. One day we will all be made perfect and be able to worship together face to face with the living God. One day, every tribe, tongue and nation will declare together the wonders of God's amazing love. Live in light of eternity today. Worship here as you will in heaven, and watch as heaven invades earth around you with the glory and love of God.

Extended Reading: Ephesians 4

Tilling the Soil of the Heart: Prayer

DAY 6

DEVOTIONAL

God makes an amazing promise to us in Philippians 4:6-7. Scripture says, *"Do not be anxious about anything, but in everything by prayer and supplication with thanksgiving let your requests be made known to God. And the peace of God, which surpasses all understanding, will guard your hearts and your minds in Christ Jesus."* How incredible! If we will make our requests known to God in prayer, giving our burdens and anxieties over to him, then he will swap those burdens for a guarding

"Do not be anxious about anything, but in everything by prayer and supplication with thanksgiving let your requests be made known to God. And the peace of God, which surpasses all understanding, will guard your hearts and your minds in Christ Jesus."

PHILIPPIANS 4:6-7

peace that surpasses all understanding. How much do you need his peace today? What areas of your life feel burdened? What do you feel anxious about?

God has an endless reservoir of peace that's available to you when you place your trust in him through prayer. As we open our hearts to God in prayer, the Spirit produces the fruit of peace. When you lay your burdens at God's feet, trusting that he will take care of you as he promised, peace overflows as a fruit of the Spirit's work in your life. That's the assurance of your Father and the power of prayer.

For most of us, something like trusting God and handing over all our burdens is much easier said than done. How can you pray effectively? How can you have communication with God? E.M. Bounds said, "The goal of prayer is the ear of God, a goal that can only be reached by patient and continued and continuous waiting upon Him, pouring out our heart to Him and permitting Him to speak to us. Only by so doing can we expect to know Him, and as we come to know Him better we shall spend more time in His presence and find that presence a constant and ever-increasing delight." Effective prayer is a process, but it is a process completely worthy of your efforts. Corrie ten Boom said, "Don't pray when you feel like it. Have an appointment with the Lord and keep it. A man is powerful on his knees." Make a daily time to set aside for prayer. Fight to keep it at all costs. Connecting to God through prayer, hearing his voice, and experiencing his presence will lead you to a satisfied life. The Christian life without prayer is no different than a relationship with a person without communication. While your God will never fail you as people do, abundant relationship with him requires constant communication.

Prayer is more about making time and space to commune with God than it is about what you do or say. God can guide, speak, and give you his presence if you simply make space for him to do so. Don't let a feeling of insecurity, doubt, or lack of knowledge keep you from talking with God. He delights in the simplicity, vulnerability, and honesty of you just wanting to talk with him.

Open your heart to God as you enter into a time of guided prayer. Make space to listen to the voice of your Helper, the Holy Spirit. And receive the wonder and peace that comes from casting your burdens on a loving Father who is waiting right now to spend time with you.

WISDOM

GUIDED PRAYER

1. Take a moment to quiet your heart and mind. Make space in your heart to allow for the peace of God to fill.

"And the peace of God, which surpasses all understanding, will guard your hearts and your minds in Christ Jesus." Philippians 4:7

2. Now lay any burdens you have at his feet. Think about anything you've been feeling anxious about, and talk to God about it. Tell him how you've been feeling.

"Humble yourselves, therefore, under the mighty hand of God so that at the proper time he may exalt you, casting all your anxieties on him, because he cares for you." 1 Peter 5:6-7

3. Now receive the peace God has promised you over those situations. Trust God that when you ask for his guidance and help, he will give it to you. Prayer changes things. While you may not be able to see it with your eyes, prayer moves the heart of God and men.

"And we know that for those who love God all things work together for good, for those who are called according to his purpose." Romans 8:28

The Bible tells us to *"rejoice always, pray without ceasing, give thanks in all circumstances; for this is the will of God in Christ Jesus for you"* (1 Thessalonians 5:16-18). The more you practice prayer and see it work in your life to bring peace and change to your circumstances, the more prayer will become a natural overflow for you. A simple thought to God at a tough or important time or even a quick act of giving God thanks for the good things around you are all are powerful, mood-altering prayers. Have a continual conversation with God and allow him to transform lonely times into continuous communion with him.

Extended Reading: Philippians 4

Tilling the Soil of the Heart: God's Voice

DAY 7

DEVOTIONAL

Spiritual father Brother Lawrence once wrote, "There is not in the world a kind of life more sweet and delightful than that of a continual conversation with God." We are meant to commune with our heavenly Father, to be in conversation with him throughout the day concerning all that's going on around us. For a long time, I held the belief that God doesn't like to talk. I thought you found out how to live the Christian life solely through reading the Bible, going to church, listening to sermons, etc. I thought prayer

"When the Spirit of truth comes, he will guide you into all the truth, for he will not speak on his own authority, but whatever he hears he will speak, and he will declare to you the things that are to come."

JOHN 16:13

was just asking God for things and waiting to see if he said yes or no through circumstances. God does speak through circumstances and his word, to be sure, but he also loves to speak directly to his children. He longs to be in conversation with us.

The Bible clearly teaches that God speaks to his people. Jesus teaches us in John 16:13 that *"When the Spirit of truth comes, he will guide you into all the truth, for he will not speak on his own authority, but whatever he hears he will speak, and he will declare to you the things that are to come."* In John 10:27 God tells us, *"My sheep hear my voice, and I know them, and they follow me."* God promises to speak to you as his child. He longs to tell you his love for you even more than you long to hear it. He longs to tell you his plans even more than you want to know them.

There hasn't been a single thing more impactful in my life than hearing the voice of God. His voice is so tender when I need tenderness, corrective when sin constricts my life, and powerful when only he can make the changes in my life that need to be made. He speaks perfectly, never a word out of place and always at the perfect time. You might hear God more than you think. I've never heard him speak audibly to me, but every day he whispers to my heart what I need to know. There are days I don't stop to listen. There are times I allow the weight of the world to crowd out his voice. But as I turn my heart back towards him, I find out that he was there—speaking all along. He whispers of his love for me when I feel crushed by the opinion of man. He tells me he's proud of me when I feel like everything I'm doing doesn't measure up. He whispers of his plans for me when I turn and go my own way. It's not because I'm gifted in some certain way that I hear his voice, but rather because God in his grace loves to speak.

God has never made a spiritually deaf person. You can hear God because his voice is immeasurably more about his love than your abilities. You are his child; his love for you is vast, unchanging and unceasing. All it takes to hear him is simply inclining an ear to him and allowing his words to take root in you. As he speaks of his love, you will feel the chains of the world fall off. As he tells you of his purpose, you will discover that a plan has been in the works for you since before you were born. Choose to listen to his voice today; let it drown out the cares of the world and create a soil in you receptive to his seed, fertile and filled with the fruit of the Spirit.

GUIDED PRAYER

1. Meditate on the truth of what the Bible says about hearing God.

"And your ears shall hear a word behind you, saying, 'This is the way, walk in it,' when you turn to the right or when you turn to the left." Isaiah 30:21

"When the Spirit of truth comes, he will guide you into all the truth, for he will not speak on his own authority, but whatever he hears he will speak, and he will declare to you the things that are to come." John 16:13

2. Now take time to listen to God. Ask him how he feels about you. Talk to him about anything that's bringing you stress. Listen for a whisper of his voice or an inclination that seems to be of God.

3. Let the truth of what he's speaking settle into your heart. Pay attention to inclinations, to longings or urgings of the Spirit. Ask him for greater understanding of what he's speaking to you. Choose to trust that he will speak and guide you into the fullness of life if you will simply follow him.

There is a practice to hearing God's voice, but it's more a practice of casting off the things of the world than anything else. Sometimes, it takes time to quiet your soul and focus on God. Don't be frustrated if you feel like you aren't hearing anything. The weight of all of this is on God. God speaks in any and every way he can. He loves to speak through the Bible and through circumstances so listen for his voice and continually seek him. There's no pressure from God. He desires to take weight and burden from us instead of putting it on. He just wants you to live in relationship with him. Let his voice settle in your heart today and become a refreshing source for you in every circumstance.

Extended Reading: John 16

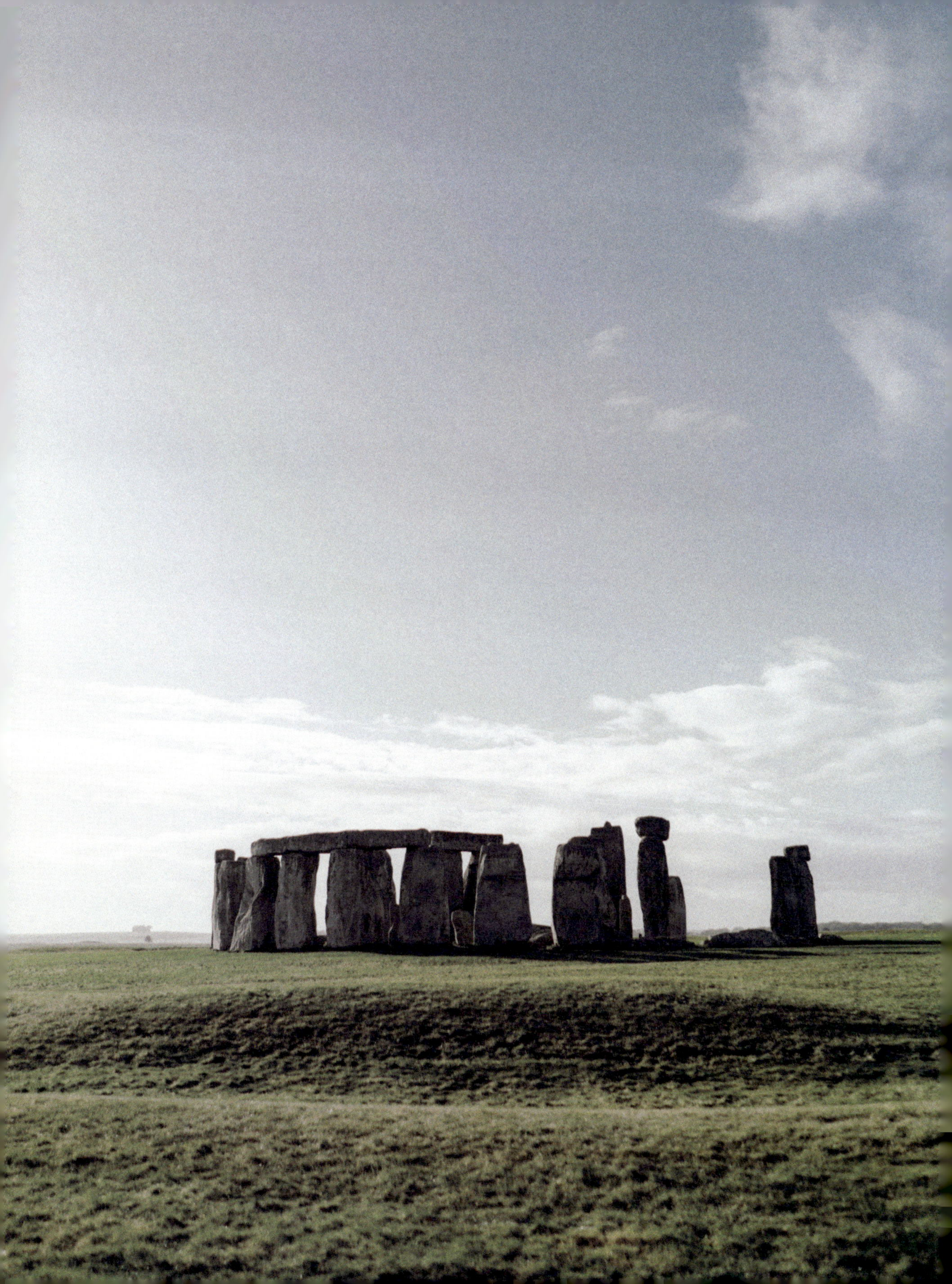

DAYS 8 - 14

The desires of every heart

02

WEEK

*"Delight yourself in the Lord,
and he will give you the desires of
your heart." Psalm 37:4*

WEEKLY OVERVIEW

All of us have insatiable desires that can only be satisfied in communion with our heavenly Father. The desire to be delighted in, for wonder, to behold beauty, and to be someone great are driving forces within each of us. The desire to be fully know and fully loved, to be passionate, and to live a life of significance resound within each of us at the foundation of who we are. God created these desires knowing that they can only be fully satisfied in him—that they would be avenues to deeper relationship with him. As we look at each of these desires individually, I pray your heart would find its fulfillment in the loving nearness of your heavenly Father.

The main concept for this week is derived from *The Seven Longings of the Human Heart* by Mike Bickle and Deborah Hiebert.

The Desire to be Delighted in

DAY 8

DEVOTIONAL

The human race has no greater driving force than the desire to be delighted in. Most of us have spent our entire lives working to be enjoyed by others. We'll go to whatever length necessary to prove ourselves worthy of being liked or loved. Some work tirelessly at a talent or skill hoping to impress with their abilities. Some devote countless hours to their appearance hoping the way they look will attract others and satisfy their desire to be delighted in. Some hope that money

> *"As a bridegroom rejoices over the bride,*
> *so your God will rejoice over you."*
>
> ISAIAH 62:5

and possessions will cause people to like them or to want to spend time with them. Regardless of how we seek to be liked, if we're honest, we will discover this desire is a driving force in all of us.

Think back on your life. Think back on yesterday. What did you do so that people would like you—so that people would like you? I could name lots of ways I strive for people's affection or adoration on a daily basis! I desire with everything in me to be delighted in. I cringe at the thought of feeling cast out, loved by too few or none—unenjoyable. You see, we can't help our need to be delighted in because God created each of us with desires that match avenues he's created to lead us back to his presence.

Our Father created all of us with a desire to be delighted in by *him*. The Creator of all things, the only one who knows everything about you, longs for you to know that he deeply enjoys you. You, just being fully you, are loved. You, with all your failures, victories, sins, and quirks are loved by God. God made you the way he did for a reason! He savors talking with you, and watching you work. He longs for you to live the life he's laid out for you and experience the fullness of joy he has richly provided you. Of course he hates when we sin. He can't possibly approve of something we're doing that's harmful to us and others. But even in our failure God pursues us. Even in rebellion God longs for us to turn our hearts toward him so that he can run out to meet us and clothe us with grace. Out of his unconditional love, he wants to throw a celebration in honor of restored relationship with you (Luke 15:11-32).

Seek fulfillment for your desire to be delighted in in the arms of your loving Father. See him as your Father running out to meet you that you might be fully loved by him. Let his love sink into the depths of your heart that your desire to be delighted in may be fully satisfied in him. May your time in guided prayer be marked by the joy your Father has over you.

GUIDED PRAYER

1. Open your Bible to Luke 15:11-32 and meditate on the story of the prodigal son. Put yourself in the story and place your perception of God in the character of the father. Ask the Spirit to help you see yourself in the story, to believe God's word about yourself.

2. Now ask the Spirit to show you how God feels about you right now. Ask him to show you how God the Father rushes towards you and longs to wrap you up in his arms.

"The Lord your God is in your midst, a mighty one who will save; he will rejoice over you with gladness; he will quiet you by his love; he will exult over you with loud singing." Zephaniah 3:17

3. Receive the delight of your heavenly Father. Rest in the love of God and let it fill up the depths of your heart.

"For God so loved the world, that he gave his only Son, that whoever believes in him should not perish but have eternal life." John 3:16

When you feel the urge to do something to gain the approval of man today, stop and receive God's delight again. Doing life out a place of already being delighted in is the only way to live emotionally fulfilled. You have an abundantly full reservoir of love available to you at any time. God is always pleased to show you how much he loves you if you will simply turn your heart toward him and receive. May your day today be marked by the limitless love of your heavenly Father.

Extended Reading: Luke 15

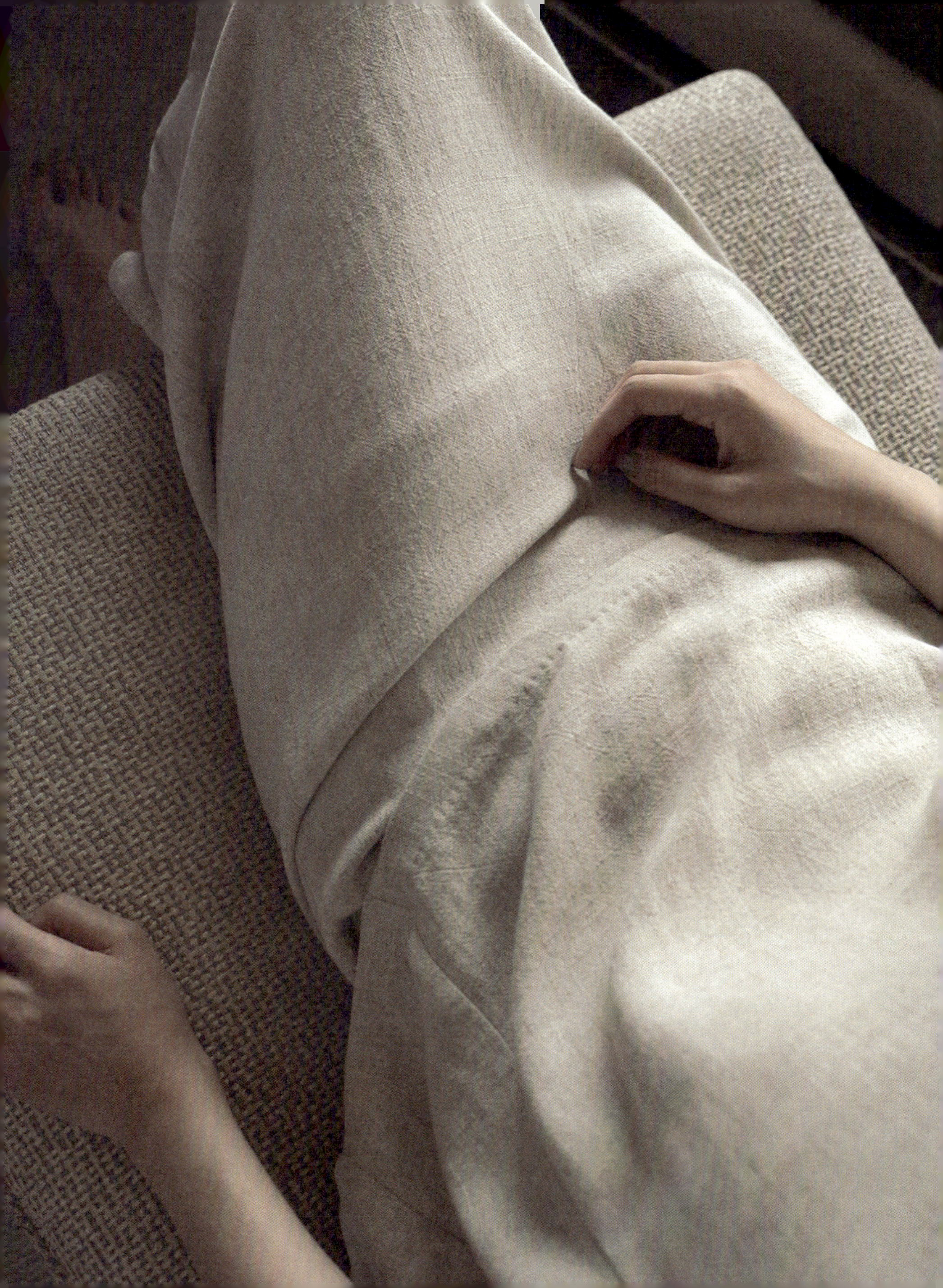

The Desire for Wonder

DAY 9

DEVOTIONAL

All of humanity is marked by an insatiable desire for wonder. We long for that which is unexplainable, intensely interesting, and unfathomable. But too often we settle for being temporarily fascinated by the things of the world. We look at concepts, cultures, and man-made creations and wonder in that which is meant to lead us to the One who is most wonderful—our heavenly Father.

WEEK 2

"Claiming to be wise, they became fools, and exchanged the glory of the immortal God for images resembling mortal man and birds and animals and creeping things."

ROMANS 1:22-23

You and I were created to marvel at the invisible nature and miraculous, supernatural works of God. We were created to know personally the God who created a universe so vast that its enormity is beyond measure. We're created to experience communion with the God who created that which is so miniscule even our largest microscopes can't capture it. We serve a God of wonder who alone can satisfy our insatiable desires for fascination.

But somewhere along the way we've chosen as a people to seek to wonder in the world over God. Romans 1:22-23 gives us insight into this destructive pursuit. Scripture says that early on in history humans *"claiming to be wise... became fools, and exchanged the glory of the immortal God for images resembling mortal man and birds and animals and creeping things."* Sin turned our gaze from God to his creation. We exchanged that which would wholly fascinate us for all of eternity for idols that were never designed to satisfy us at all. You can see it all around. In our culture, we idolize the created over the Creator. We lift up men and women instead of looking to the King of kings. We spend hours placing our hope in that which will never fully satisfy us. I can see it in myself. I jump from material thing to material thing, TV show to TV show, idea to idea, just looking for something to fascinate me. I'll be fascinated with something for a week or month at most, and then I get bored. We buy and sell, get in and out of relationships, and ride emotional roller coasters, the whole time thinking, "This will be it; this is what I'm missing."

God is calling us to a restored life where our need for wonder is satisfied in him—producing peace, joy, fulfillment and purpose. He is calling us to stop seeking to marvel in that which is fleeting and to root ourselves in him who is eternally satisfying. He is calling us to look at the world through a heavenly perspective to see that all of his creation, good or bad, would draw us to himself.

Take some time in guided prayer to assess the ways in which you are seeking satisfaction for your desire for wonder. May you wholly marvel at your present, eternal, and loving heavenly Father today.

WISDOM

GUIDED PRAYER

1. Assess your own heart. Where do you seek wonder? Are you looking to the created or the Creator to satisfy your desire to be fascinated?

2. Ask the Holy Spirit to help you explore the depths of God. Have faith in God's word:

"These things God has revealed to us through the Spirit. For the Spirit searches everything, even the depths of God." 1 Corinthians 2:10

"It is the glory of God to conceal things, but the glory of kings is to search things out." Proverbs 25:2

3. Ask God to teach you something new about himself. Ask him to show you how he desires to satisfy your need for wonder.

"Because of your unfailing love, I can enter your house; I will worship at your Temple with deepest awe." Psalm 5:7 (NLT)

"Ascribe to the Lord the glory due his name; bring an offering and come before him! Worship the Lord in the splendor of holiness." 1 Chronicles 16:29

God designed the world in such a way that it would direct us back to him. He wants you to be fascinated with your spouse, nature, ideas, creation, and even entertainment, as long as they direct you back to their true source! He wants to amaze you both through the works of his hands and in spending time with him in meditation, worship, study of the word, and simply listening as he speaks. He's designed so many wonderful avenues with which to satisfy your desires—just don't get caught up with the created things themselves. May God satisfy your desire for wonder today and every day. May he remain the source of your wonder and awe. The choice is up to you! What will you spend your time and energy seeking today?

Extended Reading: Romans 1

The Desire to Behold Beauty

DAY 10

DEVOTIONAL

Beauty is captivating in all its forms. From sunsets to mountain tops, flower petals to starry nights, we devote countless hours, years, and even lives to the wonder and pursuit of beauty. We write songs and poetry in devotion to that which inspires us with its beauty. We spend our blood, sweat, and tears in attempt to discover if we have any beauty within ourselves. We are a people marked by a need for beauty—an insatiable desire that can only be satisfied in its Creator.

*"For the Lord takes pleasure in his people;
he will beautify the humble with salvation."*

PSALM 149:4 (AMP)

For a long time I tried to rid myself of the desire for beauty. I tried simply not to want it. I equated this desire within me to a pursuit of vanity that seemed only to end in destruction. It wasn't until my desire for beauty began to find its satisfaction in God that I discovered God's original purpose behind it.

The desire to behold beauty is an incredible gift given to us by our heavenly Father. Every time we look upon something beautiful we get a glimpse into the beautiful heart of God. Our God is a perfect creator who makes beautiful things. Everything he is and does is beautiful in its own way. So when you feel a desire to be beautiful or see beauty, you are really feeling a desire for the Almighty, Triune God. You were created with an insatiable need to look upon your Creator in all his power and glory that you might stand in awe of his indescribable beauty for all eternity. And you have a longing to hear the voice of your heavenly who calls you lovely no matter how you look in the world's eyes or what you've done.

Psalm 27:4 says, *"One thing have I asked of the Lord, that will I seek after: that I may dwell in the house of the Lord all the days of my life, to gaze upon the beauty of the Lord and to inquire in his temple."* May we pursue the beauty of God and live in the glorious freedom of boundless communion with him. May our questions of whether we are beautiful find total fulfillment in the perfect perspective of he who shines forth in perfect beauty. And may we find satisfaction in all that is beautiful by acknowledging beauty that exists because of our beautiful God—limitless and perfect in all he does.

Take time in guided prayer to look upon your Creator. Gaze at the beauty of the Trinity. Let him tell you how he sees you. Listen as he speaks into the deepest recesses of your heart and satisfies places the world could never even reach. He longs for you to know how beautiful you are to him. He longs for you to stand in awe of the wonders of his perfect, true, and unconditional love. May your time be marked by clear revelation from the Holy Spirit into the heart of God.

GUIDED PRAYER

1. Take time to meditate on what the Bible says about God's beauty.

"Splendor and majesty are before him; strength and beauty are in his sanctuary." Psalm 96:6

"One thing have I asked of the Lord, that will I seek after: that I may dwell in the house of the Lord all the days of my life, to gaze upon the beauty of the Lord and to inquire in his temple." Psalm 27:4

"And above the expanse over their heads there was the likeness of a throne, in appearance like sapphire; and seated above the likeness of a throne was a likeness with a human appearance. And upward from what had the appearance of his waist I saw as it were gleaming metal, like the appearance of fire enclosed all around. And downward from what had the appearance of his waist I saw as it were the appearance of fire, and there was brightness around him. Like the appearance of the bow that is in the cloud on the day of rain, so was the appearance of the brightness all around. Such was the appearance of the likeness of the glory of the Lord. And when I saw it, I fell on my face, and I heard the voice of one speaking." Ezekiel 1:26-28

2. Ask the Spirit to reveal to you how God sees you. Ask for a revelation of your beauty to him.

"And you, who once were alienated and hostile in mind, doing evil deeds, he has now reconciled in his body of flesh by his death, in order to present you holy and blameless and above reproach before him." Colossians 1:21-22

"I am my beloved's, and his desire is for me." Song of Solomon 7:10

"O my dove, in the clefts of the rock, in the crannies of the cliff, let me see your face, let me hear your voice, for your voice is sweet, and your face is lovely." Song of Solomon 2:14

3. Take time to rest in the truth of God's heart.
Allow his thoughts to sink into your heart. Journal how God sees you and how it makes you feel.

The more you behold the beauty of the Lord and receive the knowledge of his perspective, the more you will experience freedom and unshakable joy. You are beautiful in his sight. Nothing can change the fact that you are fully loved by a perfect God. Rest in the peace and joy of that truth today. May his love lay a firm foundation for you to live secure and unshakable as your desire for beauty is wholly satisfied.

Extended Reading: Psalm 149

WEEK 2

The Desire to be Great

DAY 11

DEVOTIONAL

As children, we dream of a life of adventure and impact. We pretend to be astronauts adventuring into the unknown, police officers serving and seeking justice, or even a king rightly deserving respect from all in our kingdom. No child ever

> *"What no eye has seen, nor ear heard, nor the heart of man imagined, what God has prepared for those who love him."*
>
> **1 CORINTHIANS 2:9**

dreams of doing something mundane or meaningless. But as we grow older, we accept reality—that few ever attain what society deems the most respected and honorable professions. We settle into mediocrity and work to attain greatness in whatever ways we can. We give our lives to a business, a social circle, or even a church position all in an attempt to fulfill our need to do something or be someone great.

The truth is that our desire to be great will never be satisfied until we surrender our concept of greatness to the truth of Scripture. Jesus tells us, *"Whoever humbles himself...is the greatest in the kingdom of heaven"* (Matthew 18:4). And in Matthew 20:26 Jesus says, *"Whoever would be great among you must be your servant."* You have a heavenly Father who longs to make you great in his sight. He has a plan for you filled with eternal reward, significance and satisfaction. But it will cost you everything. His plan is the exact opposite of the world's. To be eternally great is to lay down your life, stop seeking greatness in the world's eyes and give your heart entirely to the service and plans of your heavenly Father.

The Bible tells of the wonderful life in store for those who would devote themselves to the Lord. Matthew 5:19 tells us that *"...whoever does them and teaches them [God's commandments] will be called great in the kingdom of heaven."* 1 Corinthians 2:9 says, *"What no eye has seen, nor ear heard, nor the heart of man imagined, what God has prepared for those who love him."* In John 10:10, Jesus proclaims that he came to earth in order that we might have *"life, and have it abundantly."*

The opinion of man is fleeting and fickle. But your heavenly Father's plans and purposes are entirely steadfast. You can live a life so great that all of eternity is changed as a result. You can live your life so devoted to God that heaven meets earth through your life and changes the eternal trajectory of souls.

You were made to be great. You are called to a specific task that only you can do. Take time to surrender your life entirely to your heavenly Father as you enter into guided prayer. May your time be marked by the peace, passion and purpose that comes from wholeheartedly living for God.

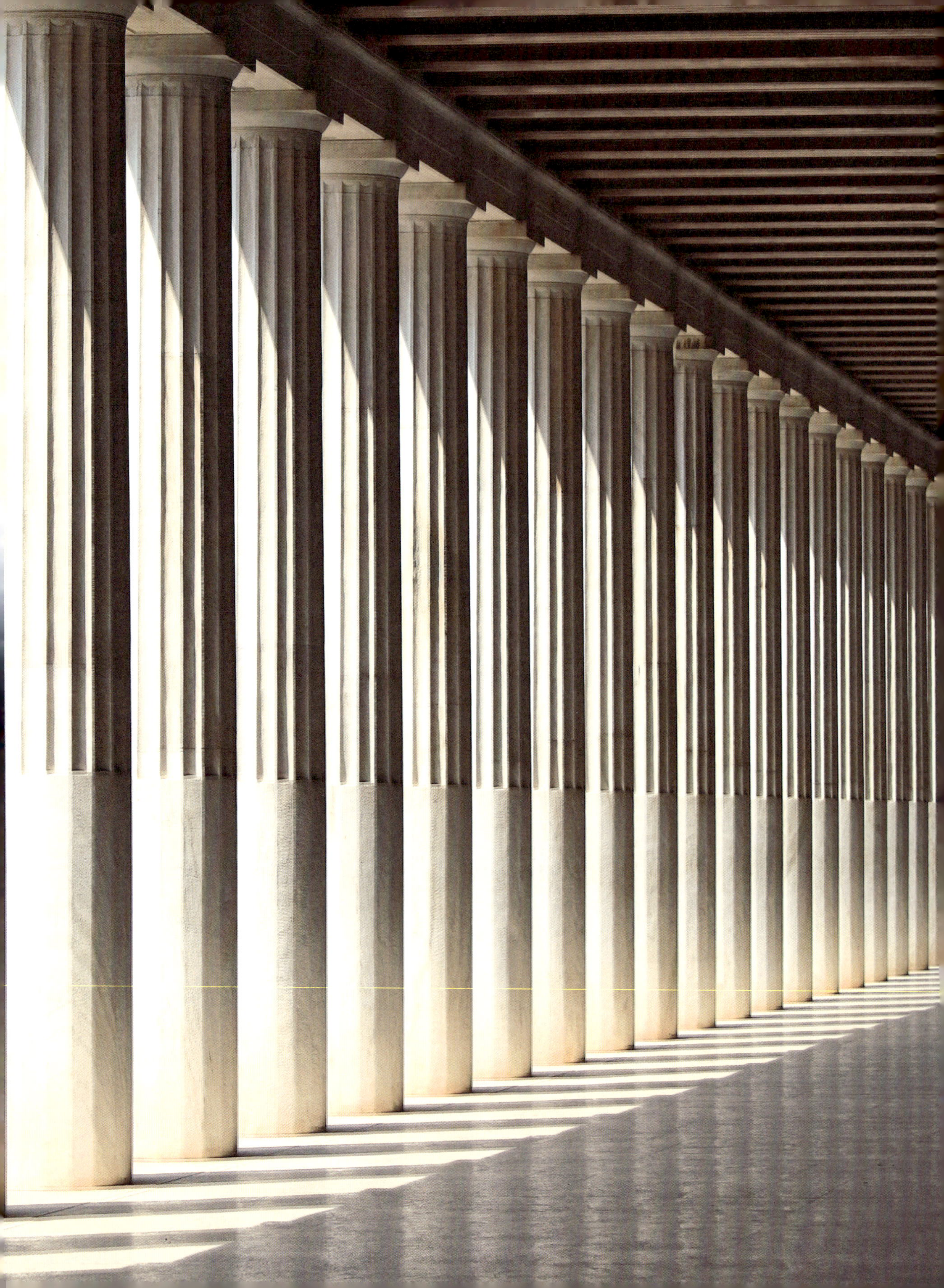

GUIDED PRAYER

1. In what ways are you seeking to be great in the world? Take time to confess any of your pursuits that aren't in line with the heart of God as stated in Scripture.

"Whoever humbles himself...is the greatest in the kingdom of heaven" Matthew 18:4

2. Now ask God to reveal his heart for what he deems to be great in your life. Ask the Holy Spirit to instill in you a desire to lay down your life that you might find it in God.

"Do not be conformed to this world, but be transformed by the renewal of your mind, that by testing you may discern what is the will of God, what is good and acceptable and perfect." Romans 12:2

"Whoever would be great among you must be your servant." Matthew 20:26

3. Now commit yourself to live in pursuit of his opinion instead of the world around you. Ask the Spirit to help you live in line with his perfect leadership. Commit yourself to trust him as he leads you into the perfect plans of your heavenly Father.

"And your ears shall hear a word behind you, saying, 'This is the way, walk in it,' when you turn to the right or when you turn to the left." Isaiah 30:21

Follow whatever the Spirit would lead you to do today. True repentance requires us to turn away from the life we've been living and live for God instead. It always leads us to a better, more abundant life. Know that whatever the Spirit leads you to do, it is out of love for you. Responding to his leading is the only way to live a life full of the fruit of the Spirit and the only way to satisfy your desire to be great. May your day be marked by the purposes and plans of your loving heavenly Father.

Extended Reading: Ephesians 1

The Desire to be Fully Known and Fully Loved

DAY 12

DEVOTIONAL

All of humanity is in a constant search for intimacy. We devote ourselves to earning the affections of others, whether it be a close friend or a stranger. We long to be loved for who we truly are, but we've also been burned by others in attempt to find acceptance. We give our hearts to the world and hope others will satisfy our craving for acceptance—for love. And we've been rejected by the very people and systems in which we sought satisfaction. Still we

> *"But God, being rich in mercy, because of the great love with which he loved us, even when we were dead in our trespasses, made us alive together with Christ."*
>
> **EPHESIANS 2:4-5**

press on. We mold and reshape ourselves; we change our image or personality. We project who we think we should be instead of who we are. We project who we feel others want us to be—believing the lie that who we really are isn't enough. And all the while we long to be fully known and accepted. We desire to be fully seen and free of guilt or shame.

This depiction holds true for all of us, because all of us have been affected by Adam and Eve's original sin. It was in perfection that they chose sin over unfettered, boundless relationship with the Father. And Scripture says in Genesis 3:8 that Adam and Eve *"heard the sound of the Lord God walking in the garden in the cool of the day, and the man and his wife hid themselves from the presence of the Lord God among the trees of the garden."* After God calls out to Adam and Eve, Adam responds by saying, *"I heard the sound of you in the garden, and I was afraid, because I was naked, and I hid myself"* (Genesis 3:10). Sin immediately and tragically brought shame, separation and destruction to perfect intimacy.

And so often we live our lives as if Scripture stopped with Genesis 3:10. We live our lives apart from the revelation of God's unconditional love and affection for us. Genesis 3:21 tells us, *"The Lord God made for Adam and for his wife garments of skins and clothed them."* God created a covering for their shame. He met them in their weakness and provided for them. And just as God covered Adam and Eve with garments to cover their shame, he's made a way for us today. In our weakness and shame God meets us and calls us lovely. He's clothed us with the perfect, righteous nature of Christ. Our lives are perfectly hidden in his. In his grace he wraps his arms around us and tells us of his great love. He speaks truth where lies have resounded. He speaks life where there seemed to only be death. He brings light to the darkest, most desolate places of our hearts. Only his grace abounding could lead us back into the fold of his loving kindness. Redemption and love fill the weak frame of man with the glory of God. We are dust transformed into the very likeness of the living God. Our destiny will always be to be fully loved and fully known by our perfect Father.

Take time in guided prayer to assess your own heart. In what ways are you still hiding from God as Adam and Eve did? In what ways have you veiled your heart as if God didn't already rip the veil separating him from us in two? May your time in guided prayer be filled with new levels of intimacy as you allow God to fully know you and bring light to darkness.

GUIDED PRAYER

1. Take time to acknowledge any shameful places in your life you've hidden from God and others. In what ways are you veiling your heart? What do you long to keep in darkness?

2. Now meditate on God's love for you. God loves you completely no matter what you've done. He longs to be with you no matter how ashamed you might feel.

"But God, being rich in mercy, because of the great love with which he loved us, even when we were dead in our trespasses, made us alive together with Christ." Ephesians 2:4-5

"No, in all these things we are more than conquerors through him who loved us. For I am sure that neither death nor life, nor angels nor rulers, nor things present nor things to come, nor powers, nor height nor depth, nor anything else in all creation, will be able to separate us from the love of God in Christ Jesus our Lord." Romans 8:37-39

3. Open your heart to God. Talk to him about any shameful places in your life. Receive a revelation of his unconditional love. Allow him to bring his healing light to your heart as you rest in his love.

Allowing ourselves to be fully known is always scary. We fear that if we are fully known and then rejected we'll have nothing left to hold on to. But until we allow ourselves to be fully known it will be impossible to satisfy our desire to be fully loved. Opening your heart, your past, your weaknesses, and your failures to God is the only path to healing and freedom. Allowing God to reveal his unconditional love for you when you've opened up about your worst pain, thoughts, and sins will fill you with a love and security you never knew was possible. Open your heart to your loving heavenly Father today and experience the love that can only come with being fully known.

Extended Reading: Ephesians 2

WEEK 2

The Desire to be Passionate

DAY 13

DEVOTIONAL

Passionate devotion, love, and purpose captivate us. As a culture we cling to stories like *Romeo and Juliet, Gone with the Wind, Don Quixote, The Count of Monte Cristo and Les Miserables* for the passionate actions of the characters. These stories evoke within each of us a desire to be equally passionate in our own lives. We long to give ourselves completely to something or someone that our lives might have true purpose.

> *"And you shall love the Lord your God with all your heart and with all your soul and with all your mind and with all your strength."*
>
> **MARK 12:30**

Humanity is captivated by passion because we were created for it. God created us with a desire to be passionate that he might satisfy that desire with his plans. The Bible is the ultimate story of passion. It's the story of God coming down to us and giving himself completely for us to the point of death. Defeating death, he now desires to use us as passionate children to lead the whole world to salvation and freedom that our lives would impact eternity.

You were made to be passionate, but oftentimes church is the last place you think of as passionate and wholehearted. So often, we in vocational ministry are scared to lose our volunteers and congregation by asking too much of them, so we never present them with an opportunity to live as passionately as God intends. The truth is that God wants all of you. He's calling you to a life of passionate surrender everywhere you go. He doesn't want to meet you just at church, at a gathering of believers, or even in your personal times; he wants you all day every day. God's calling you to a life of adventure in which the outcome is only known by him. He's calling you to step out of everyday living to a life of staggering surrender so great that this world will no longer feel like home. The call is worthwhile. His presence is worth the cost. God has a story for the ages prepared just for you—a story with real, eternal impact. But it will cost you everything to live it.

If this truth sounds radical to you, it's because it is. So many Christians will never live out the fullness of what God planned for them because of how radical it sounds. Fear grips us; we choose the comfortable path with minimal impact. But if we follow this compromise to its end, we will live passionless, mediocre lives in which we are never fully satisfied. We will live in this gap where one moment we worship God and the next we seek satisfaction in sin. We will live vicariously through the stories we hear in movies, books, and television of people who lived passionately. And at the end of our lives, we will look back and wish we had another chance to live for what really matters.

But you have a choice today. A radical life of passionate love for God awaits you. It's waiting for you right now. It doesn't mean you have to pack your bags and head out on the mission field. It doesn't necessarily mean you have to lead someone to Jesus today. It could be as simple as opening your heart fully to God and allowing him to fill you with his love to overflowing. Commit your life to him in full surrender today. Respond to his leadership with a continual "yes" in your heart. Give yourself to him completely that your life would be marked by a passionate pursuit of the perfect, pleasing and powerful plans of your heavenly Father.

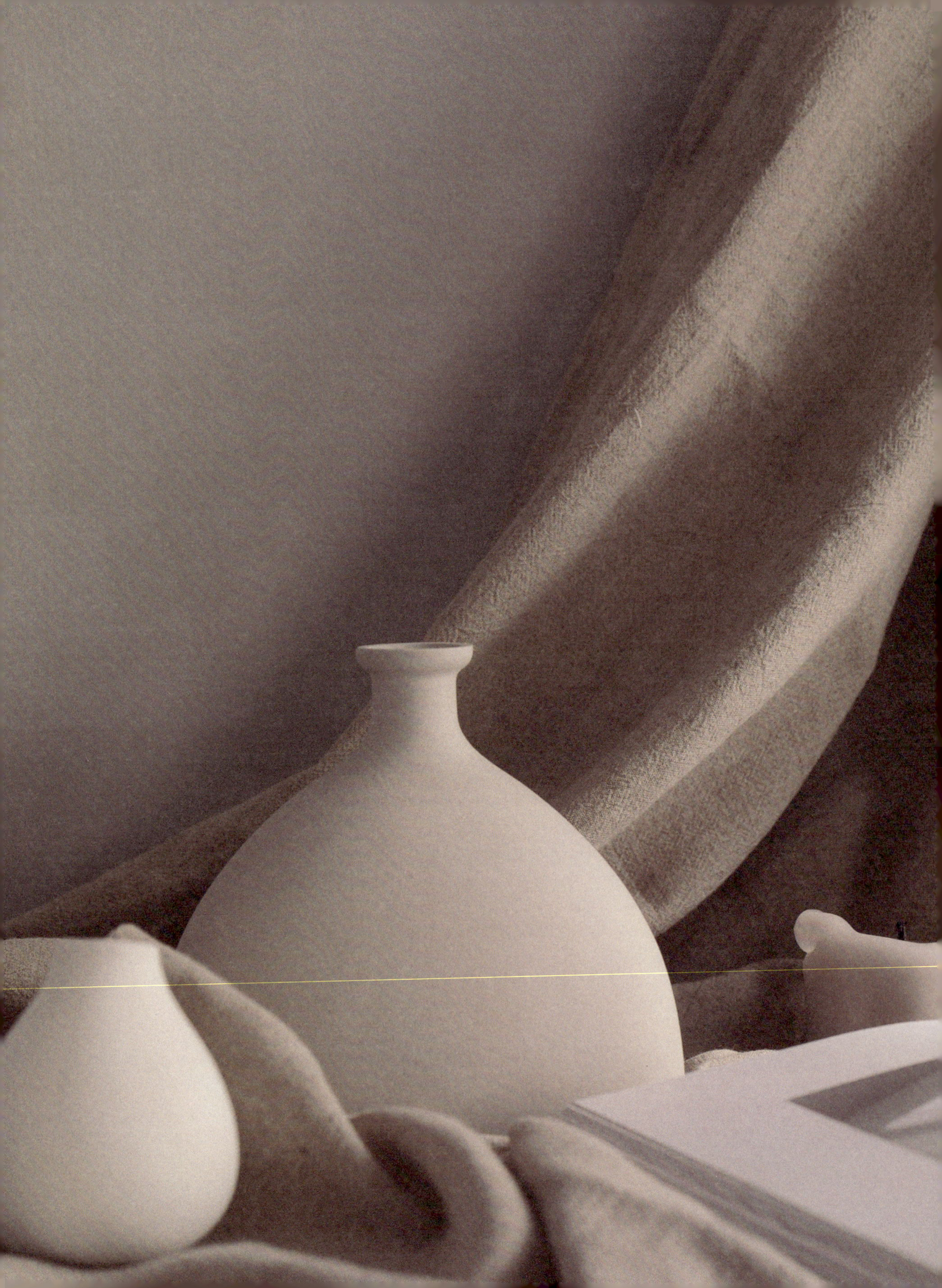

GUIDED PRAYER

1. Take a minute to meditate on Jesus's passionate pursuit of you. Think about how he lived and died to make a way for relationship with you.

"In this the love of God was made manifest among us, that God sent his only Son into the world, so that we might live through him. In this is love, not that we have loved God but that he loved us and sent his Son to be the propitiation for our sins." 1 John 4:9-10

2. Now ask God to reveal to you how he wants you to live passionately today. He has a plan each day for you; one that will give you joy, passion, and peace on a whole new level you've yet to experience. There's more for you everyday.

3. Ask the Spirit to help you live the life God has shown you. Ask him to fill you with a desire to be obedient and passionate in response to God's love. Ask him to help you be aware of what he's speaking to you and to walk in full obedience to it. Take time to rest in the presence of God.

You have an enemy that has been lying to you about who you are. Satan tells us we are weak, fearful, and unable to live sold out to anything but comfort. He pinpoints our fears and flaws in attempt to keep us from responding to the call of God. But greater is he that is in you (1 John 4:4)! If God calls you to something, he has and will continue to see you through it. *"And I am sure of this, that he who began a good work in you will bring it to completion at the day of Jesus Christ"* (Philippians 1:6). The Bible is full of stories of men and women who were weak and felt unprepared but chose to believe God at his word rather than give in to reservation. Whatever lie you've been told, trust God and ask him to correct it. Choose to believe God's word over that which contradicts it. And watch as his plans for you come to wholehearted fulfillment.

"Let us hold fast the confession of our hope without wavering, for he who promised is faithful." Hebrews 10:23

Extended Reading: 1 John 4

The Desire to Live a Life of Significance

DAY 14

DEVOTIONAL

People often ask a common question when it looks like their time on earth is drawing to a close—"Did my life matter?" Have you ever wondered that? Have you ever taken a minute to look back on your life and wonder if all your efforts will mean a thing when you're gone?

We all dream of being a great success. No children playing sports in their backyard fantasize about hanging up the towel after high school. They dream of making it pro. No

> *"Well done, good and faithful servant. You have been faithful over a little; I will set you over much. Enter into the joy of your master."*
>
> **MATTHEW 25:21**

musician dreams about playing to a handful of people. They see themselves on a massive stage in front of thousands of screaming fans. We all have a desire to make an impact in this world. We all desire to make a difference to the degree that we will be remembered when we're gone.

God designed us all with this desire while having the perfect plan to satisfy it. The problem is that we have twisted what success really looks like. We've made success into something prideful—an idea constrained to the ways of this world. We've been living under the notion that living a life of significance is all about ourselves. You see, making an impact doesn't necessarily mean you're known by the entire population, have books written about you, or are even a success at all in the eyes of the world. Success is solely defined by God and solely achieved by your faithfulness to whatever he has called you to. You are meant for the significance that faithfulness to God brings, not an impact wrought with struggle for achievement by the world's standards.

The Bible clearly defines success as being faithful to what God has spoken. In Matthew 25:21 God says, *"Well done, good and faithful servant. You have been faithful over a little; I will set you over much. Enter into the joy of your master."* Your desire to make an impact will only be satisfied by living in obedience to God's will for you. It's his plan we're all a part of, not our own. God has brought us into the glorious narrative that has been playing out from the foundation of the earth. Being faithful to your page in God's grand narrative has an eternal significance more important and long-lasting than anything you could achieve on your own. One day, all of the grand stories of what mankind has done in pursuit of our own glory will be brought to nothing. One King will stand above all. Jesus Christ will be given his reward, and we will reign alongside him forever.

Choose to live a life of significance for eternity today. Be faithful first to love God and then to love others with compassion and humility. You have a chance to lead people into eternal life. You have a chance to store up your treasure in heaven where moth and rust will not destroy (Matthew 6:19-20). You have a chance today to cause change and significance beyond anything you could imagine. Allow God to define your identity and purpose. Experience the joy and fulfillment that can only be found in passionate communion with your heavenly Father.

GUIDED PRAYER

1. Take a moment to reflect on the life of Jesus. Allow what Scripture says about Jesus to establish a true definition of success.

"Have this mind among yourselves, which is yours in Christ Jesus, who, though he was in the form of God, did not count equality with God a thing to be grasped, but emptied himself, by taking the form of a servant, being born in the likeness of men. And being found in human form, he humbled himself by becoming obedient to the point of death, even death on a cross." Philippians 2:5-8

2. Take a moment to surrender your notion of success and impact, and center your life around God's truth.

3. What plans does God have for you today? How can you love him and others well? In what way can you impact eternity?

Jesus is the perfect example of what it looks like to live a life of significance because he was wholly surrendered to the will of the Father. At the end of his ministry, he had only a few followers that stood by him. He never wrote a book or even traveled more than a few hundred miles from where he was born. Rather than considering him successful, the world killed him. But he made the biggest impact of anyone in all of history. Live like Jesus today. Live solely for the opinion of God, and find your satisfaction in being faithful to what he has called you to. May your day be filled with the abundant life that comes from surrender to the perfect plans of God.

Extended Reading: Matthew 25

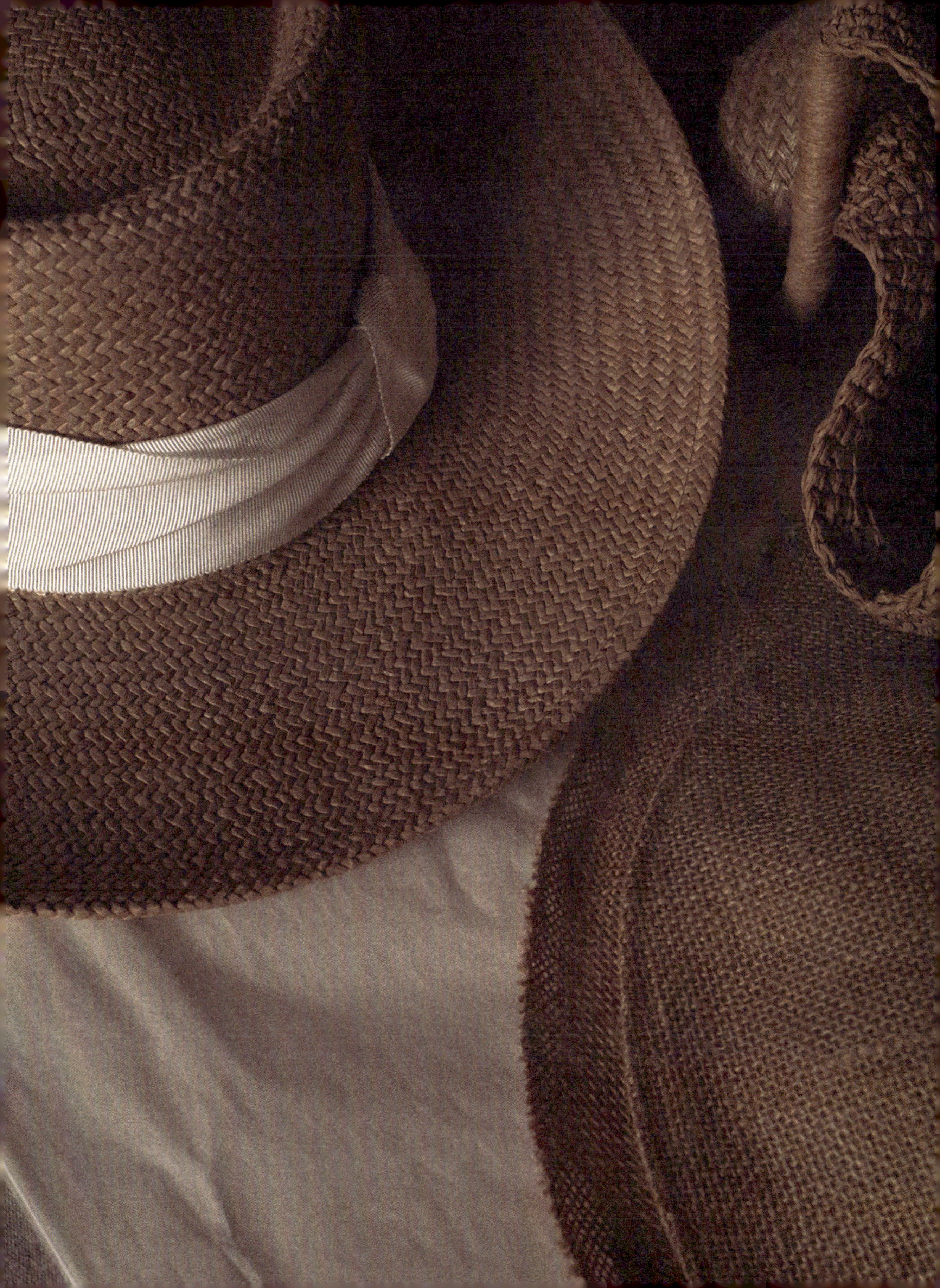

DAYS 15 - 21

Parables

03

WEEK

"For as the heavens are higher than the earth, so are my ways higher than your ways and my thoughts than your thoughts." Isaiah 55:9

WEEKLY OVERVIEW

Jesus loved to use stories to illustrate profound, life-transforming concepts. He loved to use real and genuine settings, characters, and ideas that apply to all of us to reveal God's heart of pursuit and love. This week we're going to spend time allowing the parables of Jesus to speak directly to our situations, mindsets, and core beliefs about who God is. Open your heart and mind to be transformed by the powerful and captivating stories of Jesus.

The Parable of the Good Shepherd

DAY 15

DEVOTIONAL

Have you ever experienced a sense of grand perspective where you realize your smallness in comparison to the earth's grandeur? Have you ever contemplated your small stature in light of how colossal the universe is? Every now and then, when I get a sense of my smallness I am overcome by the fear of being lost. I think, "Who will show me my path in this seemingly increasing world? Who will guide me through the various trials and changes that will undoubtedly come my way? Who will help me?"

One of my favorite metaphors in Scripture is God as the Good Shepherd. Jesus is the most equipped guide we could ever have. He holds all of creation in the palm of his hand, and yet he knows the number of hairs on our head. He is the God of the gigantic and a lover of every little detail about us. And he longs to lead us to safe pasture. As we look at the parable of God as the Good Shepherd today, allow your faith and affections to be stirred by God's promise to guide you into the matchless life he has in store for you.

John 10:14-15 says, *"I am the good shepherd. I know my own and my own know me, just as the Father knows me and I know the Father; and I lay down my life for the sheep."* Jesus paved the way for us to enter into the most amazing pasture of all: the very presence of the living God. He laid down his life as our Good Shepherd that we might eat of the fruit of his death and resurrection. But God didn't only lead us to heaven; he continually leads us as our Good Shepherd day in and day out.

In the famous Psalm 23 David writes, *"The Lord is my shepherd; I shall not want. He makes me lie down in green pastures. He leads me beside still waters. He restores my soul. He leads me in paths of righteousness for his*

"I am the good shepherd. I know my own and my own know me, just as the Father knows me and I know the Father; and I lay down my life for the sheep."

JOHN 10:14-15

name's sake. Even though I walk through the valley of the shadow of death, I will fear no evil, for you are with me; your rod and your staff, they comfort me. You prepare a table before me in the presence of my enemies; you anoint my head with oil; my cup overflows" (Psalm 23:1-6).

God's staff is meant to comfort us. As our Good Shepherd he promises to lead us daily to the plans he has for us. That doesn't always mean that we will be led out of *"the valley of the shadow of death,"* but that in the valley he will *"prepare a table before me in the presence of my enemies."* Our great comfort is the fact that God will never leave us or forsake us (Deuteronomy 31:6). As Psalm 139:9-10 says, *"If I take the wings of the morning and dwell in the uttermost parts of the sea, even there your hand shall lead me, and your right hand shall hold me."* God is with us in times of trouble. He will protect us, provide for us, and lead us to still waters.

God longs to guide you today. What trouble is before you? Where do you need guidance? Where do you need help? God promises to be your Good Shepherd. You have the most high God on your side. You can trust in his leadership. Jesus was faithful to come and die so that you might have eternal life. If he was faithful to lead you to heaven, he will certainly lead you through whatever trial you are going through now.

"Trust in the Lord with all your heart, and do not lean on your own understanding. In all your ways acknowledge him, and he will make straight your paths" (Proverbs 3:5-6). Your God is a trustworthy Shepherd. Enter into prayer with expectancy that he will guide you perfectly and in his perfect timing. Cast your cares on him and trust him. Allow him to *"make straight your paths"* as you follow the leadership of the Holy Spirit.

GUIDED PRAYER

1. Meditate on the idea of God as your Good Shepherd. Receive the truth of his promise to lead you and protect you.

"I am the good shepherd. I know my own and my own know me, just as the Father knows me and I know the Father; and I lay down my life for the sheep." John 10:14-15

"You have led in your steadfast love the people whom you have redeemed; you have guided them by your strength to your holy abode." Exodus 15:13

"If I take the wings of the morning and dwell in the uttermost parts of the sea, even there your hand shall lead me, and your right hand shall hold me." Psalm 139:9-10

2. Where do you need his leadership today? Where do you need his protection? Cast your cares on his shoulders and receive the peace that comes from trusting in him.

"Casting all your anxieties on him, because he cares for you." 1 Peter 5:7

3. Ask the Holy Spirit for leadership. Your God will directly guide you through trials. Trust in his leadership and follow whatever it is he tells you to do. If his word speaks directly to your situation, commit to obeying it! God promises to guide you as your Good Shepherd.

"This is God, our God forever and ever. He will guide us forever." Psalm 48:14

"Trust in the Lord with all your heart, and do not lean on your own understanding. In all your ways acknowledge him, and he will make straight your paths." Proverbs 3:5-6

"And I will lead the blind in a way that they do not know, in paths that they have not known I will guide them. I will turn the darkness before them into light, the rough places into level ground. These are the things I do, and I do not forsake them." Isaiah 42:16

"Now may the God of peace who brought again from the dead our Lord Jesus, the great shepherd of the sheep, by the blood of the eternal covenant, equip you with everything good that you may do his will, working in us that which is pleasing in his sight, through Jesus Christ, to whom be glory forever and ever. Amen." Hebrews 13:20-21

Extended Reading: John 10

The Parables of the Hidden Treasure and Valuable Pearl

DAY 16

SCRIPTURE

"The kingdom of heaven is like treasure hidden in a field, which a man found and covered up. Then in his joy he goes and sells all that he has and buys that field." Matthew 13:44

DEVOTIONAL

If you could only have one thing in life, what would it be? Take an honest look at your heart for a minute today. What do you love most? What would you give up everything else for?

Would you believe that your heavenly Father's answer to those questions is you? That the Creator of the universe loves you most? Would you believe he would give up everything to have relationship with you? I heard a life-changing sermon from Pastor Robert Morris of Gateway Church in which he proved, by looking at Genesis 2, that God's greatest desire is relationship with us. After God creates Adam in his own image, God says, *"It is not good that the man should be alone; I will make him a helper fit for him"* (Genesis 2:18). God brings every created animal before Adam to see if he deems any of them suitable as a helper, and Genesis 2:20 says, *"But for Adam there was not found a helper fit for him."* Then without consulting Adam, God puts him to sleep and forms a woman out of his rib. Seeing the woman upon waking, Adam says, *"This at last is bone of my bones and flesh of my flesh; she shall be called Woman, because she was taken out of Man"* (Genesis 2:23). How did God know Adam would want a woman as his helper? How did God know she would be the desire of his heart? God knew Adam most longed for a bride because Adam was made in God's image, and God's greatest desire is for relationship with us, whom the Bible calls his Bride.

Let the truth of God's heart sink in for a minute. Out of everything else God has created or could have created, he most desires relationship with you. And he so longed for you to know him fully that he sent Jesus to die to make restored relationship possible. God calls us to himself daily with his love. He stands at the door of our heart and knocks, beckoning us with his loving-kindness to simply come and know him.

Once we truly grasp the depth of God's desire for us, the only true response is to give up everything for him. He laid the foundation for our commitment to him with the greatest single act of love, and he simply waits, beckoning us to respond, living our lives with him as our highest priority. And he doesn't do so selfishly, but because the absolute best way for us to live our lives is in total commitment to him.

In Matthew 13:44-46, Jesus tells a parable explaining this response to God's unending love. He says, *"The kingdom of heaven is like treasure hidden in a field, which a man found and covered up. Then in his joy he goes and sells all that he has and buys that field. Again, the kingdom of heaven is like a merchant in search of fine pearls, who, on finding one pearl of great value, went and sold all that he had and bought it."* The kingdom of God is the greatest treasure, the pearl of greatest value. Relationship with him is worth our entire lives. Pursuing him with all our heart is the absolute greatest ambition we could have. Paul described this pursuit in Philippians 3:8 when he said, *"Indeed, I count everything as loss because of the surpassing worth of knowing Christ Jesus my Lord. For his sake I have suffered the loss of all things and count them as rubbish, in order that I may gain Christ."*

So again, reflect on your own heart. What do you value above all else? God's not angry with you if it truly isn't him. You see, the truth is that our pursuit of God will only ever match our revelation of his goodness. God knows that if he isn't truly the greatest desire of your heart, it's because you don't fully know how good he is. If you had the full revelation of his love for you, living totally for him wouldn't even be a choice. So great is the worth of knowing Jesus that as you see him, you will naturally give up everything to know him more.

So, today as you enter into prayer, know the first step in growing in your pursuit of God is acknowledging the posture of your own heart. How strongly do you desire deeper relationship with him? How much would you give up to know him? What do you seek fulfillment in during your free time?

The second step is receiving a fresh revelation of his incredible love for you. Spend time simply encountering his heart. Meditate on the truth that he desires relationship with you above all else. He so greatly enjoys you that he pursues you with all of his focus and energy.

Last, respond to a revelation of his love with your own love. Worship him, adore him, and live for him with your life. You will encounter him in anything you do as worship. He will pour out his presence, favor, and blessing in any area you live out of love for him. Colossians 1:13-14 says, *"He has delivered us from the domain of darkness and transferred us to the kingdom of his beloved Son, in whom we have redemption, the forgiveness of sins."* And Luke 12:31 promises us, *"Instead, seek his kingdom, and these things will be added to you."*

Pursue a deeper relationship with your heavenly Father today through prayer. As you live for him and seek his kingdom first, you'll discover all he has longed to add to your life.

GUIDED PRAYER

1. Reflect on your own life. How strongly do you desire deeper relationship with him? How much would you give up to know him? What do you seek fulfillment in during your free time?

"The Lord looks down from heaven on the children of man, to see if there are any who understand, who seek after God." Psalm 14:2

2. Meditate on the depth of God's love for you. Receive a fresh revelation of how greatly he enjoys you. Think about the story in Genesis of how God's greatest desire was relationship with his Bride.

"Looking to Jesus, the founder and perfecter of our faith, who for the joy that was set before him endured the cross, despising the shame, and is seated at the right hand of the throne of God. Consider him who endured from sinners such hostility against himself, so that you may not grow weary or fainthearted." Hebrews 12:2-3

"O my dove, in the clefts of the rock, in the crannies of the cliff, let me see your face, let me hear your voice, for your voice is sweet, and your face is lovely." Song of Solomon 2:14

3. Respond to God's love with your own. Spend time simply adoring him. Spend time in solitude sitting with him, encountering his heart, and giving him your own. He paid the highest price for you just to be able have a relationship with him. So take time and be the reward of his sacrifice.

"You will seek me and find me, when you seek me with all your heart." Jeremiah 29:13

May we answer the call to live for love with our lives today. May we live in response to this benediction found in Hebrews 12:28:

"Therefore let us be grateful for receiving a kingdom that cannot be shaken, and thus let us offer to God acceptable worship, with reverence and awe."

Extended Reading: Philippians 3

WEEK 3

The Parable of the Mustard Seed

DAY 17

DEVOTIONAL

Jesus tells a beautiful parable of the kingdom of God in Matthew 12:31-32. He teaches, *"The kingdom of heaven is like a grain of mustard seed that a man took and sowed in his field. It is the smallest of all seeds, but when it has grown it is larger than all the garden plants and becomes a tree, so that the birds of the air come and make nests in its branches."* Trees are beautiful pictures of God's ability to take what we view as weak or insignificant, a seed, and make a magnificent and life-giving creation out of it. And Matthew 12 reveals how trees can be viewed as pictures of the very kingdom of their Creator. It's remarkable that God would begin his kingdom small and grow it by his faithful stewardship into a beautiful and life-giving creation.

God took the seed of the death of one man, Jesus, to create a beautiful tree of salvation for all of humanity. John 3:17 says, *"For God did not send his Son into the world to condemn the world, but in order that the world might be saved through him."* Our heavenly Father's wrath over our sin poured out on Jesus allowed God to free the rest of us from eternal condemnation. And through the seed of Jesus' death, God has been creating a powerful and eternal global movement, bringing people to restored relationship with himself across thousands of years. Just as the mustard seed grows large enough to become a tree in which birds make their home, the kingdom of God has transferred our citizenship to a new home with him. Philippians 3:20 says, *"But our citizenship is in heaven, and from it we await a Savior, the Lord Jesus Christ."* John 15:19 says, *"If you were of the world, the world would love you as its own; but because you are not of the world, but I chose you out of the world, therefore the world hates you."* The kingdom of God established through Christ has saved us from slavery to this world and ransomed us back into restored relationship with our heavenly Father.

Not only does the parable describe the incredible expanse of God's kingdom from a few to many, it can also illustrate the seed of salvation planted within each of us that God intends to grow into a beautiful and

> *"The kingdom of heaven is like a grain of mustard seed that a man took and sowed in his field. It is the smallest of all seeds, but when it has grown it is larger than all the garden plants and becomes a tree, so that the birds of the air come and make nests in its branches."*
>
> MATTHEW 13:31-32

fruit-bearing tree. Luke 17:21 says, *"The kingdom of God is in the midst of you."* God's kingdom is not built of brick and mortar, but of human hearts. And 1 Peter 2:2 commands us, *"Like newborn infants, long for the pure spiritual milk, that by it you may grow up into salvation."* God's desire is to water the seed of salvation he's planted in us with the Spirit and the word. He longs to mold and shape us into the likeness of Jesus, that we might live lives that bear incredible life-giving fruit. Hosea 14:4-7 illustrates God's heart beautifully when it says, *"I will heal their apostasy; I will love them freely, for my anger has turned from them. I will be like the dew to Israel; he shall blossom like the lily; he shall take root like the trees of Lebanon; his shoots shall spread out; his beauty shall be like the olive, and his fragrance like Lebanon. They shall return and dwell beneath my shadow; they shall flourish like the grain; they shall blossom like the vine; their fame shall be like the wine of Lebanon."* God wants to constantly steward this gift of salvation in each of us, as he does with the global advancement of his kingdom, that we might bear the wonderful fruit of the Spirit in every area of our lives.

And God is so patient with us. The earth illustrates his patience. Trees grow year after year, season to season by his faithful stewardship. Flowers never begin as beautiful as they are in full bloom. The earth is constantly undergoing abundant transformation as God's creation grows and changes. You and I are no different. God's plan has always been to mold us into beautiful pictures of his love. He's always longed to fashion us until we walk in full, restored relationship with him. And by the life and death of Christ, he's paved the way for his desires to come to fruition. All that's left is for us to engage fully in this wonderful process he's created for us. Engage in the growth he longs to birth in you by spending time in his presence and his word. Allow his gaze to transform you into his likeness. Live in obedience to the word, and allow it to lead you to an unconformed life in this world. Follow the guidance of the Spirit as he brings healing to your heart and fruit in your life.

Spend time in prayer allowing God to work in your heart today.

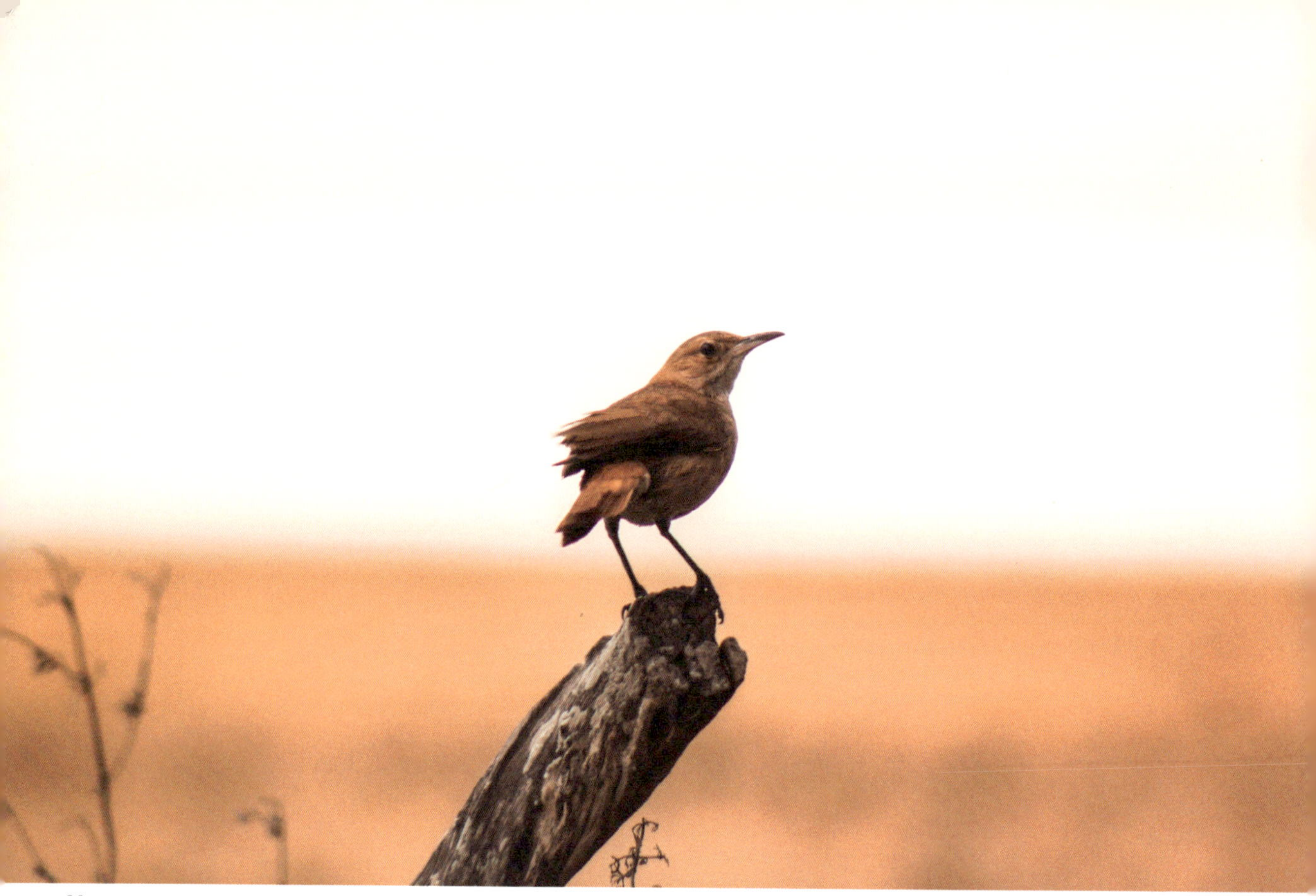

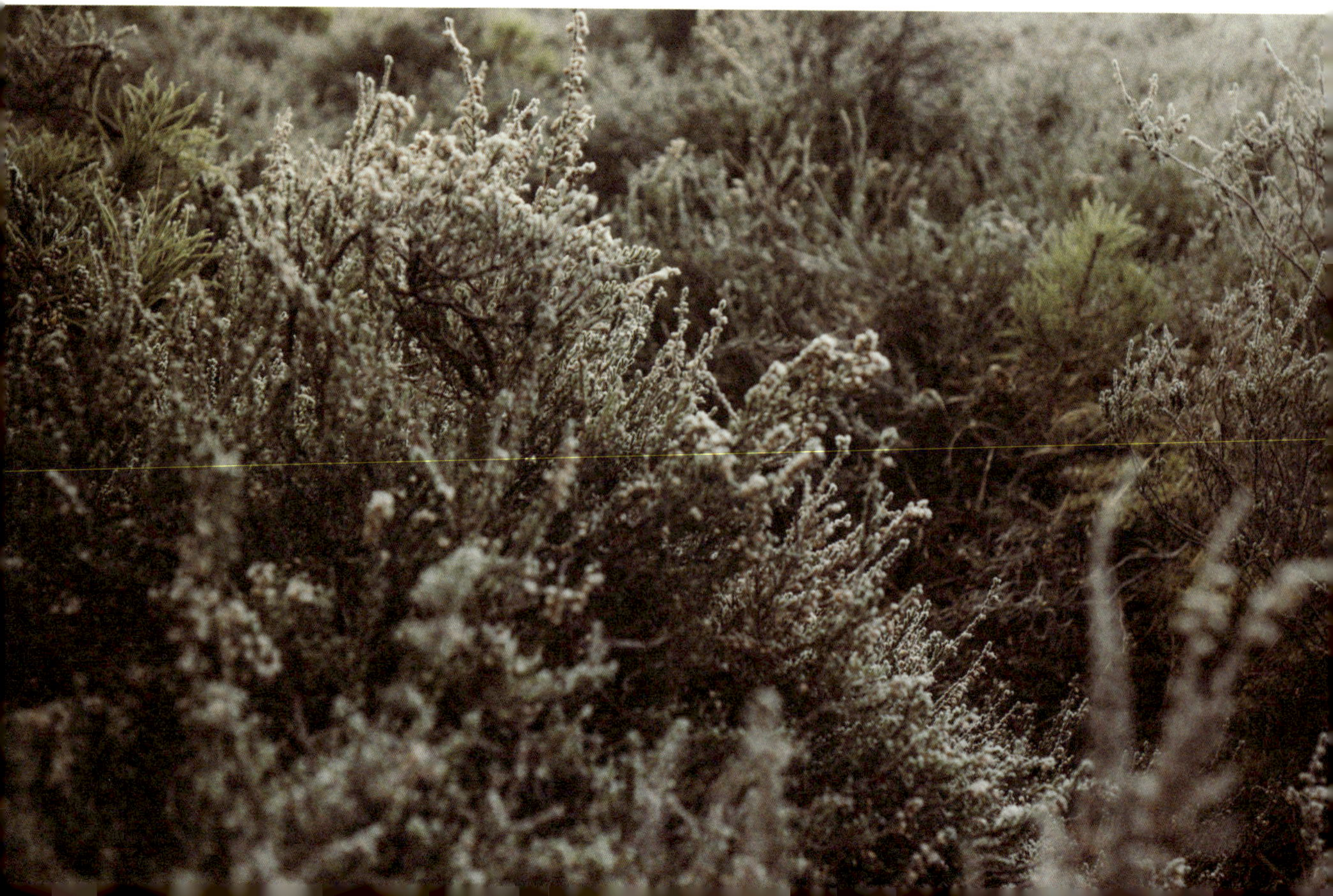

GUIDED PRAYER

1. Meditate on God's desire to grow the seed of salvation he's planted within you.

"I will heal their apostasy; I will love them freely, for my anger has turned from them. I will be like the dew to Israel; he shall blossom like the lily; he shall take root like the trees of Lebanon; his shoots shall spread out; his beauty shall be like the olive, and his fragrance like Lebanon. They shall return and dwell beneath my shadow; they shall flourish like the grain; they shall blossom like the vine; their fame shall be like the wine of Lebanon." Hosea 14:4-7

2. Where do you need growth in your own life? Where do you need to bear more fruit?

3. Ask the Spirit to fill you anew today. Be filled with the presence of God and allow his love to mold and shape you into his likeness. Ask the Spirit to guide you into areas in where he wants to grow you today. Find Scripture that pertains to those areas in which you need growth and live in obedience to God's word.

"And we all, with unveiled face, beholding the glory of the Lord, are being transformed into the same image from one degree of glory to another. For this comes from the Lord who is the Spirit." 2 Corinthians 3:18-19

How great is God's love for us that he doesn't leave us where we are but is always transforming us! In the blink of an eye, God sees who we've been, who we are, and who we will be. He knows your form, how he's created you, and what you were born to do. The more time you spend allowing him to transform you, the more you will understand yourself. May you discover and engage with all that your heavenly Father wants to do in you through his love today.

Extended Reading: 2 Corinthians 3

The Parable of the Lamp on a Stand

DAY 18

DEVOTIONAL

Reading Matthew 5:14-15 used to stress me out. Jesus says, *"You are the light of the world. A city set on a hill cannot be hidden. Nor do people light a lamp and put it under a basket, but on a stand, and it gives light to all in the house."* How can we with all our mistakes, misgivings, and failures be *"the light of the world?"* How could God in all his wisdom choose to use us to reveal Jesus, the only hope of eternal salvation, to a lost and dying world?

As I grow in my knowledge of God's heart, I grow in the revelation of his desire to use me. Passages like Matthew 5:14-15 used to focus my attention on my own sin and darkness rather than God's grace and love. But faithfully in his love, he guides my thoughts to what matters: the overwhelming reality of the Holy Spirit transforming me into the image of the God who created me. Today, let's allow the Spirit and the word to transform the way we view ourselves and how God in his infinite wisdom would use us to change the world.

Ephesians 2:10 says, *"For we are [God's] workmanship, created in Christ Jesus for good works, which God prepared beforehand, that we should walk in them."* At salvation your identity changed. You are now *"created in Christ Jesus."* 2 Corinthians 5:17 says it this way: *"Therefore, if anyone is in Christ, he is a new creation. The old has passed away; behold, the new has come."* You are a new creation not by your own doing, but by the powerful finished work of Christ Jesus on the cross. At salvation your sins were wiped away, cast off as far as the east is from the west. Such was the transformation that took place in your heart at salvation that you could be filled with God himself. Jesus says in John 14:16-17, *"And I will ask the Father,*

WEEK 3

"You are the light of the world. A city set on a hill cannot be hidden. Nor do people light a lamp and put it under a basket, but on a stand, and it gives light to all in the house."

MATTHEW 5:14-15

and he will give you another Helper, to be with you forever, even the Spirit of truth, whom the world cannot receive, because it neither sees him nor knows him. You know him, for he dwells with you and will be in you." God himself *"dwells with you"* and through salvation now lives inside you.

Passages like the parable of the lamp on a stand used to stress me out because I didn't understand what God wanted to reveal through me to the world. I used to think God wanted to reveal perfection in me, that I had to act perfectly to demonstrate Christ. What I didn't realize is that the greatest revelation I could give a broken and needy world is that God, through the immeasurable depth of his love, meets me in my brokenness and continually makes me whole. I realized that God, only by his grace, is taking what was lost, weak, selfish, and lonely and is filling me with unimaginable love and security through restored relationship with him. God doesn't want you to reveal perfection. He wants to reveal the fact that in your imperfection he has loved you from the beginning with an everlasting love.

Because you are weak and in need of God, you are the absolute best person to lead others to Jesus. If you act like you have everything together, as if nothing is wrong, then those distant from God will have no reason to believe God desires relationship with them. But in revealing your imperfection, in being honest and real with those around you, you will offer hope to a world that has none. You will reveal the core of the gospel: that God has incredible works prepared for those who simply come to him in need and cry out for his help. In your imperfection you are a perfect example of Jesus' love that comes only by grace.

God desires to shine the light of his love through you today in powerful ways. He longs to reveal to others how deeply he has loved you in his grace. He has incredible plans in store for you if you will simply be real with a world that desperately needs relationship with their Creator. Have the courage to be yourself and to be honest and vulnerable. Honesty is all your heavenly Father asks of you. In your honesty, God will reveal a greater love than this world has ever known. In the reality of who you are, God will shine forth hope, guiding those who are lost to the safe shores of restored relationship with him. May you find peace in the fact that God longs to use you exactly as you are. May you find purpose in the works he has set before you to do. And may you find joy in the revelation of God's immeasurable love poured out on you through his grace.

GUIDED PRAYER

1. Meditate on the depth of God's love for you. In your sin and need of him he continually shows you grace, gives you his presence, and offers you joy for your mourning.

"In this is love, not that we have loved God but that he loved us and sent his Son to be the propitiation for our sins." 1 John 4:10

"You make known to me the path of life; in your presence there is fullness of joy; at your right hand are pleasures forevermore." Psalm 16:11

"You have turned for me my mourning into dancing; you have loosed my sackcloth and clothed me with gladness." Psalm 30:11

2. Now ask the Spirit to reveal God's desire to use you today. Allow God to shift the way you see yourself. Allow him to ignite in you a passion to see those who are distant from God come to the revelation of his grace and love for them.

"You are the light of the world. A city set on a hill cannot be hidden. Nor do people light a lamp and put it under a basket, but on a stand, and it gives light to all in the house." Matthew 5:14-15

"For we are his workmanship, created in Christ Jesus for good works, which God prepared beforehand, that we should walk in them." Ephesians 2:10

3. Ask God to fill you with the grace to be courageous and honest. Ask for the strength to be real and vulnerable with others.

"But he gives more grace. Therefore it says, 'God opposes the proud, but gives grace to the humble.'" James 4:6

One of the most transformative parts of living in relationship with our heavenly Father is the freedom from having to act around others. You are fully loved, liked, and enjoyed just as you are. So great was God's desire for relationship with you that he sent his only Son to die for you. There is a new peace available to you as you live in the freedom to be fully yourself. Rest in the fact that the Creator of the universe loves and likes you. You have no reason to act. May you find security today as the love of your heavenly Father lays a sure foundation for you to live honestly and courageously.

Extended Reading: Psalm 30

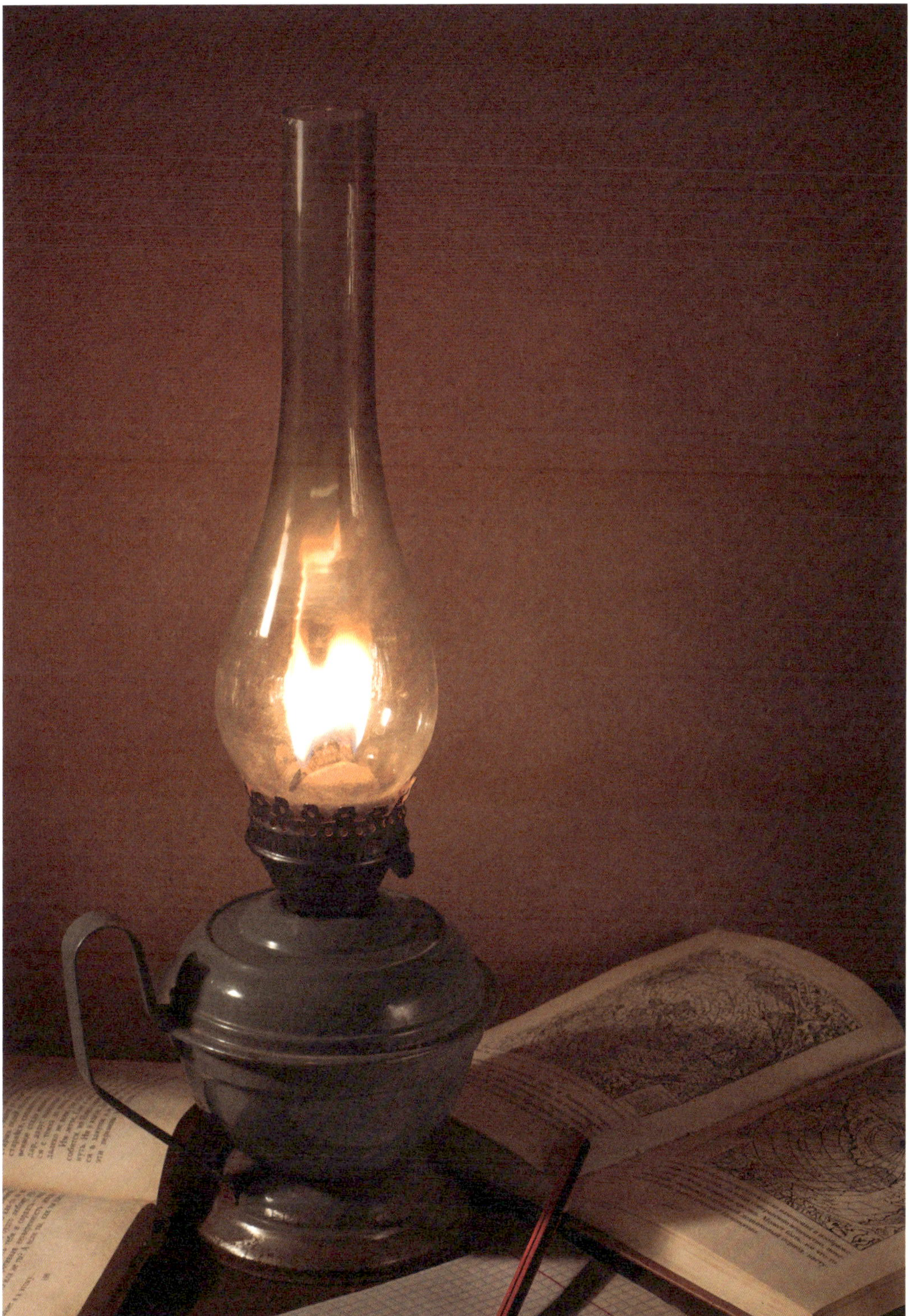

The Parable of the Pharisee and the Tax Collector

DAY 19

SCRIPTURE

"Two men went up into the temple to pray, one a Pharisee and the other a tax collector. The Pharisee, standing by himself, prayed thus: 'God, I thank you that I am not like other men, extortioners, unjust, adulterers, or even like this tax collector. I fast twice a week; I give tithes of all that I get.' But the tax collector, standing far off, would not even lift up his eyes to heaven, but beat his breast, saying, 'God, be merciful to me, a sinner!' I tell you, this man went down to his house justified, rather than the other. For everyone who exalts himself will be humbled, but the one who humbles himself will be exalted." Luke 18:10-14

DEVOTIONAL

The ministry of Jesus was one of life-giving transformation. His life, death, and resurrection ushered in a completely new way of relating to God: the way of grace. One of the best examples of Jesus shifting paradigms comes in his parable of the Pharisee and the tax collector. Luke 18:10-14 says,

Two men went up into the temple to pray, one a Pharisee and the other a tax collector. The Pharisee, standing by himself, prayed thus: "God, I thank you that I am not like other men, extortioners, unjust, adulterers, or even like this tax collector. I fast twice a week; I give tithes of

all that I get." But the tax collector, standing far off, would not even lift up his eyes to heaven, but beat his breast, saying, "God, be merciful to me, a sinner!" I tell you, this man went down to his house justified, rather than the other. For everyone who exalts himself will be humbled, but the one who humbles himself will be exalted.

Let's open our hearts and allow the Spirit to guide us to live life more like the tax collector than the Pharisee. Let's allow him to lead us to a life lived in the new covenant of grace.

In the time of Jesus, God's people were completely starved for relationship with him. Judaism had become a religion of regulations rather than relationship. God's people believed that their lives were totally based on their works, placing the religious Pharisees at the top of the totem pole stretching up to God. The Pharisees believed they were justified before God because of their works, as if they could earn their way into right standing with God. So, imagine the shock of Jesus' listeners when he says that the tax collector, the most hated of all Jews, went home justified before the Lord as the result of his humility. Imagine the shock and anger of the Pharisees in learning that all they had worked for, all the rules and regulations they had lived by, actually placed them lower in stature than any other Jew in the sight of God.

The parable of the Pharisee and tax collector offers amazing news for each of us. The principle Jesus teaches here in Luke 18 is that the greatest posture of our heart is one of humility, not perfection. The way to God is not one of works, but of grace. Jesus teaches that whatever weakness you have, whatever sin you struggle with, all God asks of you is that you come before him and ask for his mercy. All he requires of you is a repentant heart.

You see, the Lord is always after your heart. All the works of the Pharisees were birthed out of their own pride. In their egotism they thought they could earn relationship with the one, true, and holy God. All of their religious deeds were done not out of their love for God, but out of their love for their own reputation. However, the tax collector had nothing to boast about. He lived his life robbing his own people to fill the pockets of the Romans who enslaved them. He was made wealthy by stealing from his own people. But in his desperation he cried out to God for help, and God heard his cry.

Know that God hears your cry today when it comes out of the reality of your need for him. He answers your need for forgiveness and relationship with the overwhelming power of his presence. So, ask yourself today, what do you value most? Do you value your own reputation or God's opinion? Are you living in light of God's grace or trying earn it? Are you going through the motions of religion in order to earn your way into relationship with God, or are you living in response to the wealth of love you've freely received in Christ?

Wherever you are, know that it is never too late to come before your heavenly Father in humility. It is never too late to repent of any area in which pride has been your motivation and decide to live your life on the foundation of grace. It is never too late to posture your heart to receive the depths of love and mercy your heavenly Father longs to give you. Christ came to usher in the path of grace, not of works. He came so that you might live in his strength, not your own. The price of his mercy is a humble heart because humility is the key that unlocks the depths of your soul to receive the free gift of his grace. God won't fill what you believe is already full. He won't help where you don't truly believe you need him. But if you'll cry out to him and ask him for his mercy for your sin and his love to satisfy your need, he will fill your life with the gift of his unending presence.

Posture your heart like that of the tax collector as you pray. Follow his model of humility and find satisfaction for the places of your heart that are in need of God's love.

WISDOM

GUIDED PRAYER

1. Meditate on Jesus' parable of the Pharisee and tax collector. Allow the Spirit to reveal areas in which you need the help that can only be received in humility.

"Two men went up into the temple to pray, one a Pharisee and the other a tax collector. The Pharisee, standing by himself, prayed thus: 'God, I thank you that I am not like other men, extortioners, unjust, adulterers, or even like this tax collector. I fast twice a week; I give tithes of all that I get.' But the tax collector, standing far off, would not even lift up his eyes to heaven, but beat his breast, saying, 'God, be merciful to me, a sinner!' I tell you, this man went down to his house justified, rather than the other. For everyone who exalts himself will be humbled, but the one who humbles himself will be exalted." Luke 18:10-14

2. Reflect on your own life. Where are you living with the burden of pride? Where are you living in your own strength? In what ways are you building up your own reputation rather than the only one worthy of glory, Jesus? Know that any area of your life rooted in pride will be without the mercy and help of your heavenly Father. The only way to live entirely in the grace of God is in constant and true humility.

"The reward for humility and fear of the Lord is riches and honor and life." Proverbs 22:4

"Before destruction a man's heart is haughty, but humility comes before honor." Proverbs 18:12

"As in water face reflects face, so the heart of man reflects the man." Proverbs 27:19

3. Confess your sin and receive the free gift of God's presence. Cry out to God for his help in your life. Confess your need for his mercy, and take time resting in the incredible and satisfying gift of his presence. There is no greater gift in this life than spending time being with our heavenly Father. He longs to fuel you with the inexhaustible power of his nearness.

"You will seek me and find me, when you seek me with all your heart." Jeremiah 29:13

Philippians 2:3-7 says, *"Do nothing from rivalry or conceit, but in humility count others more significant than yourselves. Let each of you look not only to his own interests, but also to the interests of others. Have this mind among yourselves, which is yours in Christ Jesus, who, though he was in the form of God, did not count equality with God a thing to be grasped, but made himself nothing, taking the form of a servant, being born in the likeness of men."* If God himself lived his life in total humility, then we must follow his example in order to walk in the favor and abundance God longs to bestow on us. Look to Christ as your example, and discover God's desire to exalt you as you bow yourself before him as your Lord and King.

Extended Reading: 1 Peter 5

The Parable of the Prodigal Son

DAY 20

SCRIPTURE

"And the son said to him, 'Father, I have sinned against heaven and before you. I am no longer worthy to be called your son.' But the father said to his servants, 'Bring quickly the best robe, and put it on him, and put a ring on his hand, and shoes on his feet. And bring the fattened calf and kill it, and let us eat and celebrate. For this my son was dead, and is alive again; he was lost, and is found.'" Luke 15:21-24

DEVOTIONAL

There isn't a single passage of Scripture that better illustrates the heart of our heavenly Father than the parable of the prodigal son. So as to not miss any of the details of this life-changing passage, open your heart to the Spirit as you read it in its entirety. *And he said, "There was a man who had two sons. And the younger of them said to his father, 'Father, give me the share of property that is coming to me.' And he divided his property between them. Not many days later, the younger son gathered all he had and took a journey into a far country, and there he squandered his property in reckless living. And when he had spent everything, a severe famine arose in that country, and he began to be in need. So he went and hired himself out to one of the citizens of that country, who sent him into his fields to feed pigs. And he was longing to be fed with the pods that the pigs ate, and no one gave him anything.*

"But when he came to himself, he said, 'How many of my father's hired servants have more than enough bread, but I perish here with hunger! I will arise and go to my father, and I will say to him, "Father, I have sinned against heaven and before you. I am no longer worthy to be called your son. Treat me as one of your hired servants."' And he arose and came to his father. But while he was still a long way off, his father saw him and felt compassion, and ran and embraced him and kissed him. And the son said to him, 'Father, I have sinned against heaven and before you. I am no longer worthy to be called your son.' But the father said to his servants, 'Bring quickly the best robe, and put it on him, and put a ring on his hand, and shoes on his feet. And bring the fattened calf and kill it, and let us eat and celebrate. For this my son was dead, and is alive again; he was lost, and is found.' And they began to celebrate.

"Now his older son was in the field, and as he came and drew near to the house, he heard music and dancing. And he called one of the servants and asked what these things meant. And he said to him, 'Your brother has come, and your father has killed the fattened calf, because he has received him back safe and sound.' But he was angry and refused to go in. His father came out and entreated him, but he answered his father, 'Look, these many years I have served you, and I never disobeyed your command, yet you never gave me a young goat, that I might celebrate with my friends. But when this son of yours came, who has devoured your property with prostitutes, you killed the fattened calf for him!' And he said to him, 'Son, you are always with me, and all that is mine is yours. It was fitting to celebrate and be glad, for this your brother was dead, and is alive; he was lost, and is found'" (Luke 15:11-32).

The life-changing core of the gospel is that when we feel far from God, he is never far from us. The moment we turn back toward him, he runs out to meet us. The moment we lower ourselves in response to our sin, he exalts us, calls us his child, and throws a party in our honor. Sometimes the most important truths are the simple ones. Sometimes the very word we need most is the truth we've heard thousands of times. My prayer for you today is that you wouldn't extend yourself past the foundation of the gospel. God's desire is that we would linger in the revelation of the aftermath of Jesus' work, that through his life, death, and resurrection we have been raised to newness of life (Romans 6:4). Get lost today in the profound grace of your loving God. Of no work of your own, you have been set free from the bonds of this earth and brought back into the fold of your loving heavenly Father. Through the sacrifice of King Jesus you have been crowned as a co-heir with Christ (Romans 8:17).

Take time today to simply rest in the foundational truth of the gospel. Run toward God with all humility and allow your heart to be raised up as he exalts you. Humble yourself in light of his majesty and allow him to pour out a joy over you like you have never felt before. God has every reason to condemn you, but out of his overwhelming love he has chosen to call you his beloved child. Meditate on this life-changing truth and respond to his love with the offering of your life.

GUIDED PRAYER

1. Meditate on the profound truth of the gospel that you are fully loved only through the grace of your heavenly Father.

"For by grace you have been saved through faith. And this is not your own doing; it is the gift of God." Ephesians 2:8

"But to all who did receive him, who believed in his name, he gave the right to become children of God." John 1:12

"They shall be mine, says the Lord of hosts, in the day when I make up my treasured possession, and I will spare them as a man spares his son who serves him." Malachi 3:17

2. Where do you need to turn and run toward your heavenly Father? Acknowledge your total need of his grace and receive the abundant mercy he is waiting to pour over you.

"Blessed be the God and Father of our Lord Jesus Christ! According to his great mercy, he has caused us to be born again to a living hope through the resurrection of Jesus Christ from the dead." 1 Peter 1:3

"Let us then with confidence draw near to the throne of grace, that we may receive mercy and find grace to help in time of need." Hebrews 4:16

3. Spend time resting in the knowledge of Jesus' finished work. Rest in the love of your heavenly Father. Allow his presence and his love to change you from the inside out today. Allow the Spirit to guide you into the heart of God.

"For God so loved the world, that he gave his only Son, that whoever believes in him should not perish but have eternal life." John 3:16

There is nothing you could do that could separate you from the love of your heavenly Father. The prodigal son sinned against his father in the worst way a son could. And still the father ran out to meet him at first glance of his son's return. Your heavenly Father runs to meet you anytime you turn toward him. Don't let the enemy spread lies to you that you are too dirty for God or that you have to fix yourself before you can spend time in his presence. Your relationship with God is based completely on grace, not on works. He loves you because he loves you, not because of what you do. Go out today in the knowledge that you are eternally loved by your heavenly Father, regardless of what you do. And may his love spur you toward a life lived in the abundance of restored relationship.

Extended Reading: Romans 8

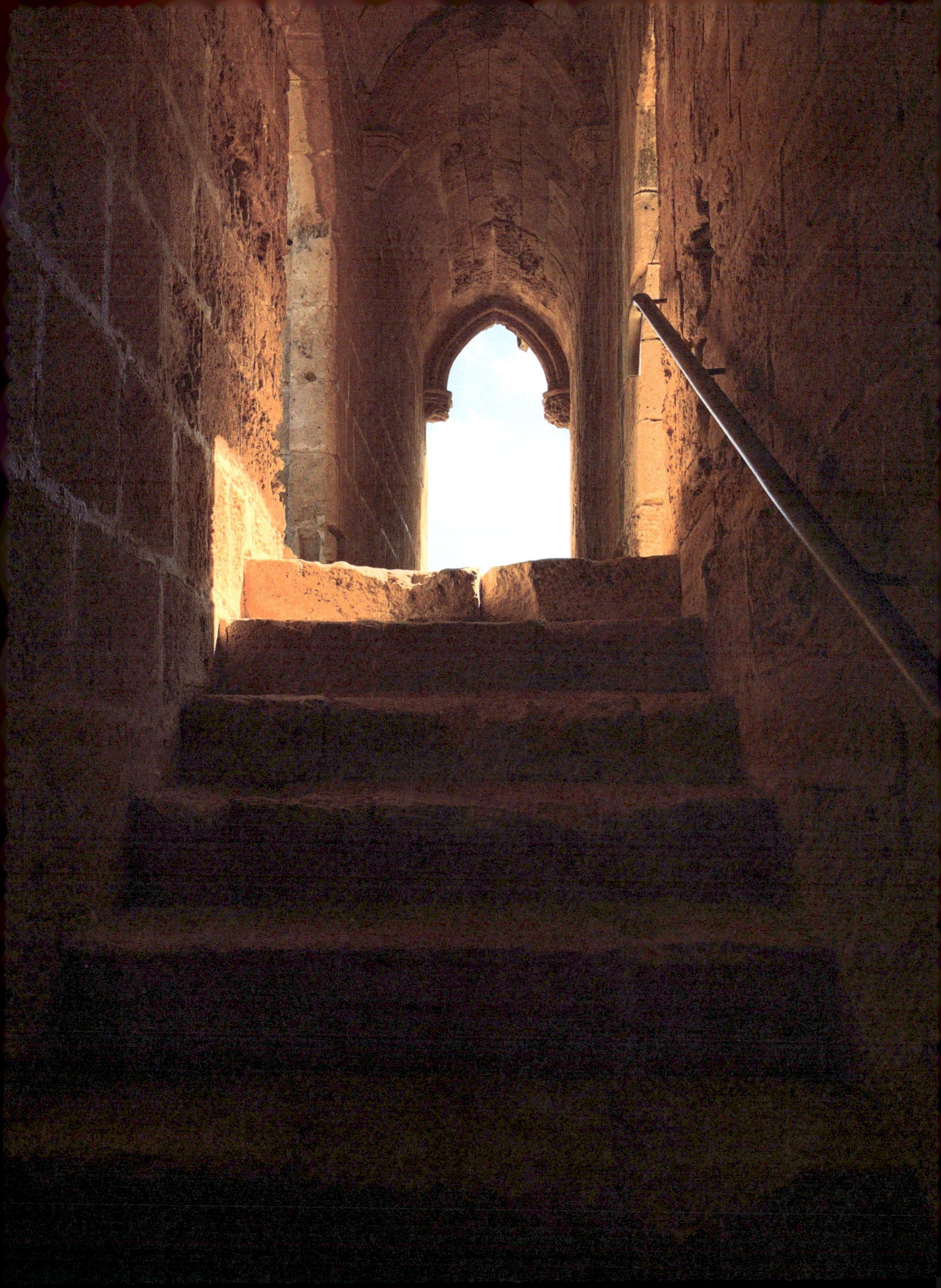

The Parables of the Lost Sheep and Coin

DAY 21

SCRIPTURE

"What man of you, having a hundred sheep, if he has lost one of them, does not leave the ninety-nine in the open country, and go after the one that is lost, until he finds it? And when he has found it, he lays it on his shoulders, rejoicing. And when he comes home, he calls together his friends and his neighbors, saying to them, 'Rejoice with me, for I have found my sheep that was lost.' Just so, I tell you, there will be more joy in heaven over one sinner who repents than over ninety-nine righteous persons who need no repentance." Luke 15:4-7

"Or what woman, having ten silver coins, if she loses one coin, does not light a lamp and sweep the house and seek diligently until she finds it? And when she has found it, she calls together her friends and neighbors, saying, 'Rejoice with me, for I have found the coin that I had lost.' Just so, I tell you, there is joy before the angels of God over one sinner who repents." Luke 15:8-10

DEVOTIONAL

If the core of Jesus' teachings on the gospel could be summed up in two stories, they would be the parables of the lost sheep and the lost coin. Both stories illustrate one crucially important truth: God pursues us. Both clearly display God's heart for us in that he willingly and passionately comes down to meet and help us wherever we are. As we look at these important parables today, open your heart and allow the reality of God's pursuit of you to transform the way you relate to him and stir up your desires to seek his face in return.

Jesus says in Luke 15:4-7,

What man of you, having a hundred sheep, if he has lost one of them, does not leave the ninety-nine in the open country, and go after the one that is lost, until he finds it? And when he has found it, he lays it on his shoulders, rejoicing. And when he comes home, he calls together his friends and his neighbors, saying to them, 'Rejoice with me, for I have found my sheep that was lost.' Just so, I tell you, there will be more joy in heaven over one sinner who repents than over ninety-nine righteous persons who need no repentance.

Then Jesus teaches in verses 8-10,

Or what woman, having ten silver coins, if she loses one coin, does not light a lamp and sweep the house and seek diligently until she finds it? And when she has found it, she calls together her friends and neighbors, saying, 'Rejoice with me, for I have found the coin that I had lost.' Just so, I tell you, there is joy before the angels of God over one sinner who repents.

Jesus tells two parables to re-emphasize a perspective-shattering truth. The One, True God, the King of kings and Lord of lords, so values us that he leaves everything behind to pursue relationship with us. So great is God's desire for restored relationship with you that he came down off his throne, left transcendent perfection, and lived his earthly life in total service to us, thereby leading him to an unjustified and sacrificial death.

Has the reality of that truth been fully realized in your heart? Has both the grandeur and love of our God hit home to the point that the depth of God's love is your chief reality? Too often we pass by the core message of the gospel because we have heard it before, and we don't allow it to stretch past our mind into our heart. It's when truth rests in our heart, impacts our emotions, and becomes real to us that it transforms our life. You were the helpless and lost sheep. You were the coin that was so valuable God worked and searched until he had it back in his possession. You are of the highest value to the only One who truly decides the essence of worth. Don't let that truth pass you by today. Instead, grab hold of it, reflect on it, and wrestle with it until it becomes the foundation for every decision, thought, and action in your life.

Let's respond to the depth of God's pursuit with our own. Let's allow God to bring every part of our lives entirely into his possession. Let's be the reward of Jesus' sacrifice. In Psalm 27:8 David says, "*You have said, 'Seek my face.' My heart says to you, 'Your face, Lord, do I seek.'*" God is calling out to you, saying, "*Seek my face.*" He waits patiently for your reply, excited at the notion that you would live your life receiving the abundance made available to you by Jesus' sacrifice.

Spend time in prayer meditating on God's pursuit of you and responding to him by seeking his face.

GUIDED PRAYER

1. Meditate on the powerful, core truth found in the parables of the lost sheep and the lost coin. Meditation is an effective way to take knowledge and allow it to sink into our hearts. Rest in the truth of Jesus' teaching.

"What man of you, having a hundred sheep, if he has lost one of them, does not leave the ninety-nine in the open country, and go after the one that is lost, until he finds it? And when he has found it, he lays it on his shoulders, rejoicing. And when he comes home, he calls together his friends and his neighbors, saying to them, 'Rejoice with me, for I have found my sheep that was lost.' Just so, I tell you, there will be more joy in heaven over one sinner who repents than over ninety-nine righteous persons who need no repentance." Luke 15:4-7

"Or what woman, having ten silver coins, if she loses one coin, does not light a lamp and sweep the house and seek diligently until she finds it? And when she has found it, she calls together her friends and neighbors, saying, 'Rejoice with me, for I have found the coin that I had lost.' Just so, I tell you, there is joy before the angels of God over one sinner who repents." Luke 15:8-10

2. Ask the Spirit to guide you into a time of response. How can you seek God's face? What can you do to offer your life as the reward for Jesus' sacrifice?

"But from there you will seek the Lord your God and you will find him, if you search after him with all your heart and with all your soul." Deuteronomy 4:29

"The Lord is good to those who wait for him, to the soul who seeks him." Lamentations 3:25

3. In faith seek God today. God promises you his presence, his nearness. He longs to guide you into real relationship with him where he satisfies your deepest desires. As you seek him, allow him to fill you up with the power and love of his presence.

"And without faith it is impossible to please him, for whoever would draw near to God must believe that he exists and that he rewards those who seek him." Hebrews 11:6

"The young lions suffer want and hunger; but those who seek the Lord lack no good thing." Psalm 34:10

"You have said, 'Seek my face.' My heart says to you, 'Your face, Lord, do I seek.'" Psalm 27:8

The chief characteristic that marks those who live life in the Spirit is their continual pursuit of God. Psalm 34:10 promises us that *"those who seek the Lord lack no good thing."* God will always respond to your pursuit of him because his greatest desire is relationship with you. You don't have to be scared to seek him, wondering if you will find him to be real and responsive. He's already promised that to you. Take Hebrews 11:16 and live your life in obedience to his word. Have faith and believe that he *"exists and that he rewards those who seek him."* May you discover a deeper reality of his nearness, love, and pursuit of you today as your respond to God's word in faith.

Extended Reading: Psalm 27

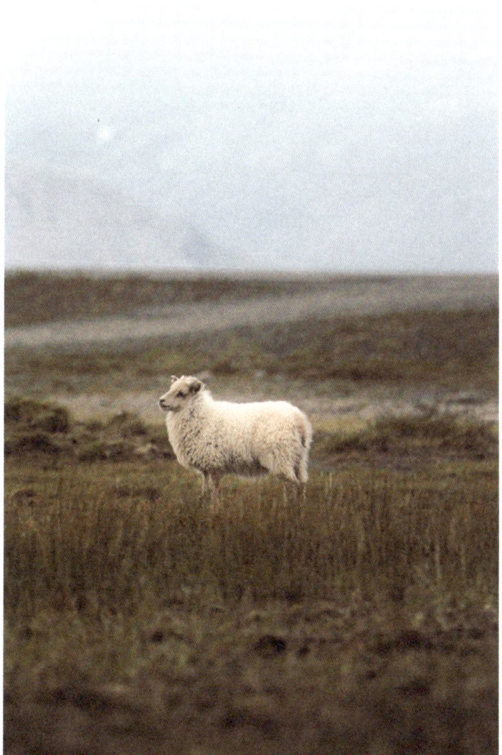

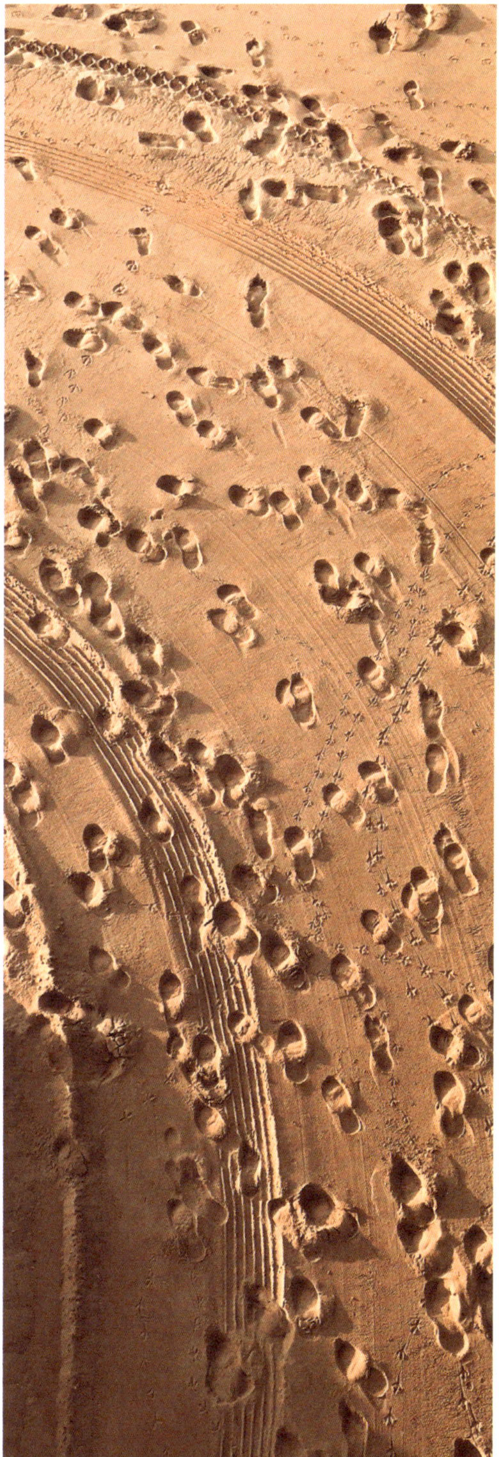

DAYS 22 - 28

Vision and boundaries

04

WEEK

"For each will have to bear his own load." Galatians 6:5

WEEKLY OVERVIEW

We serve a God of boundaries. In his limitless capacity, endless creativity, and boundless existence he still chose to create boundaries. He still had vision for what was good, right, pleasing, and perfect. And as children made in his image, we are to live, think, and create as he does. In a world marked by busyness from seemingly infinite opportunities, it's important now more than ever for us to create boundaries. May you find freedom and joy this week as you receive vision and set boundaries under the leadership of the Holy Spirit.

Being a Person of Vision

DAY 22

DEVOTIONAL

The world we live in constantly bombards us with attempts to define who we are and what we should do. Advertisements tell us what we need. Our jobs tell us how we should spend our time and find a sense of self-worth. Our families and friends often define us by what we've done or said in the past.

> *"Where there is no prophetic vision the people cast off restraint, but blessed is he who keeps the law."*
>
> **PROVERBS 29:18**

And even our churches sadly define us according to how we can best meet the needs of the church rather than getting to know who we truly are.

But we serve a God who knows us even better than we know ourselves. Psalm 139:1-4 says, *"O Lord, you have searched me and known me! You know when I sit down and when I rise up; you discern my thoughts from afar. You search out my path and my lying down and are acquainted with all my ways. Even before a word is on my tongue, behold, O Lord, you know it altogether."* And then later in verse 16 David writes, *"Your eyes saw my unformed substance; in your book were written, every one of them, the days that were formed for me, when as yet there was none of them."*

From the foundation of the earth, God knew he would make us. On the day we took our first breath he already had perfect, pleasing plans for us. He's known our every thought and looked upon our every action with grace. We could not be more known than we are by our heavenly Father. And there couldn't be a better guide through the chaos of this life than the Holy Spirit.

To be a person with healthy, life-giving boundaries starts with being a person of vision. And the only place to get true vision is from the only One who truly knows you. God longs to be the north on your compass. He longs to give you honest insight into how he's made you. He longs to give you a sense of how he sees you and feels about you. And in receiving a revelation of who you are you will be better equipped to follow his leadership into his perfect and pleasing will.

Begin this week of vision and boundaries by meeting with your heavenly Father in prayer. May you be overwhelmed by a fresh revelation of how loved you are—just as you are.

WISDOM

GUIDED PRAYER

1. Meditate on the simple truth that God truly knows you. Allow Scripture to lead you to a place of faith and trust in God's knowledge of you.

"O Lord, you have searched me and known me! You know when I sit down and when I rise up; you discern my thoughts from afar. You search out my path and my lying down and are acquainted with all my ways. Even before a word is on my tongue, behold, O Lord, you know it altogether." Psalm 139:1-4

"Your eyes saw my unformed substance; in your book were written, every one of them, the days that were formed for me, when as yet there was none of them." Psalm 139:16

2. Ask God to give you a revelation of how he sees you. Ask him for a revelation of his nearness and love. Begin to talk to him about any insecurities you have.

"Are not two sparrows sold for a penny? And not one of them will fall to the ground apart from your Father. But even the hairs of your head are all numbered. Fear not, therefore; you are of more value than many sparrows." Matthew 10:29-31

3. Ask God for a revelation of what he has called you to. Ask him about your role in your family and his calling on your life as a spouse, child, or parent. Ask him for vision for your work. Ask him for vision for your relationship with him. Journal his responses.

"For the gifts and the calling of God are irrevocable." Romans 11:29

"To this end we always pray for you, that our God may make you worthy of his calling and may fulfill every resolve for good and every work of faith by his power, so that the name of our Lord Jesus may be glorified in you, and you in him, according to the grace of our God and the Lord Jesus Christ." 2 Thessalonians 1:11-12

Often in my life I feel like a horse with blinders just putting my head down and running as fast as I can to only end up right back where I started. God doesn't desire to put blinders on us. He doesn't treat us just as tools to accomplish tasks. He's about relationship with us. He's about guiding us in having vision for our lives. He longs to help us see ourselves, this world, and opportunities before us as he does that we might gain wisdom and insight. Choose to be a person of vision. Choose to pick your head up and put on the lens of the Holy Spirit. Ask God questions. Inquire of him about your life and opportunities. And in response he will provide the leadership you need, exactly how you need it.

Extended Reading: Psalm 139

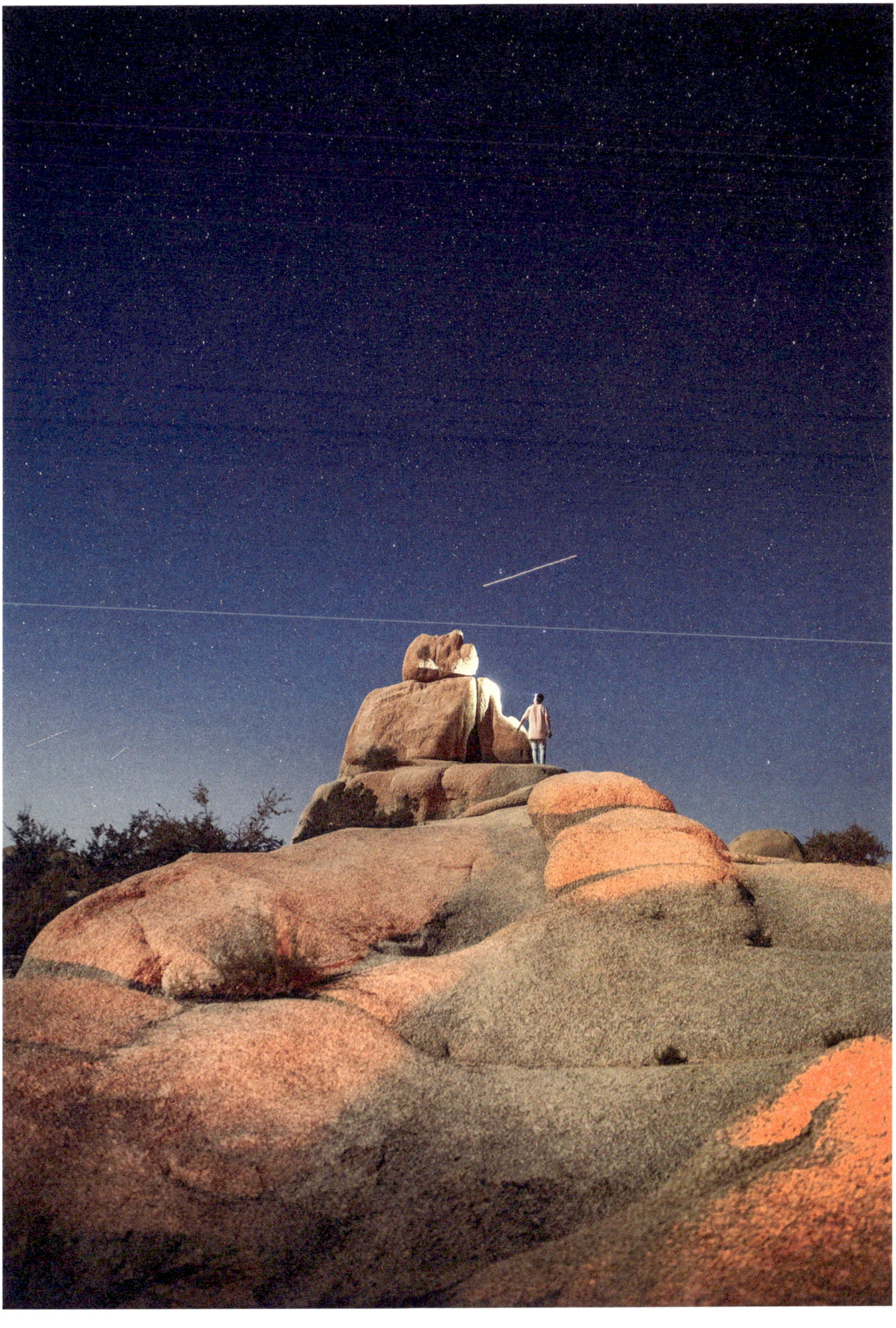

Vision for God

DAY 23

DEVOTIONAL

You were created to spend time with God. Just as God's chief desire is for relationship with you, your chief purpose in life is relationship with him. There is no life apart from him. Scripture says in Acts 17:28, *"In him we live and move and have our being."* As we seek to be a people of vision and boundaries, let's begin by looking at a passage of Scripture in which Jesus tells us the one thing that's necessary. Luke 10:38-42 says,

*"Abide in me, and I in you. As the branch cannot
bear fruit by itself, unless it abides in the vine,
neither can you, unless you abide in me."*

JOHN 15:4

"Now as they went on their way, Jesus entered a village. And a woman named Martha welcomed him into her house. And she had a sister called Mary, who sat at the Lord's feet and listened to his teaching. But Martha was distracted with much serving. And she went up to him and said, "Lord, do you not care that my sister has left me to serve alone? Tell her then to help me." But the Lord answered her, "Martha, Martha, you are anxious and troubled about many things, but one thing is necessary. Mary has chosen the good portion, which will not be taken away from her."

If I came up to you and asked you what one thing is necessary, what would your response be? If I even asked you for the one thing Jesus says is necessary, what would your response have been? Jesus destroys my value system with two sentences: *"Martha, Martha, you are anxious and troubled about many things, but one thing is necessary. Mary has chosen the good portion, which will not be taken away from her."* Allow that truth to settle in for a minute. One thing is necessary. One thing is required: to sit at the feet of Jesus. Above everything I could do for him, he wants me to sit at his feet. Above providing for my family or serving my church, he wants me to sit at his feet.

If there is one thing we need to have vision for, it is our relationship with God. Would Jesus say that you are choosing the good portion? Or would he say that you are *"anxious and troubled about many things."*

Are you spending your time investing in that which Jesus promises you will never be taken away from you? Or are you investing your life in that which won't have value past your time here.

If there is one thing to set boundaries around, it's your time spent communing with the Father. I find myself far more concerned about whether or not I show up to work on time than I do to my dedicated time with God. I find myself far more anxious and troubled about my relationship with others than I do about my relationship with Jesus. If it's really true that only one thing is necessary, we need to fight for that one thing above all else. We need to devote ourselves to sitting at the feet of Jesus above every other pursuit.

It astounds and blesses me beyond words to serve a God who longs for who I am more than what I can do. It stirs my heart to know that more than Jesus wants me to do something for him, he wants me to sit with him. Know today that in everything God is after your heart. He doesn't need your service. He doesn't need your money. He doesn't need anything at all. God can and will accomplish everything he sets out to accomplish. What he's after is life-giving, unhindered relationship with you.

Spend time today doing the one thing that's necessary: sitting at the feet of your loving Savior.

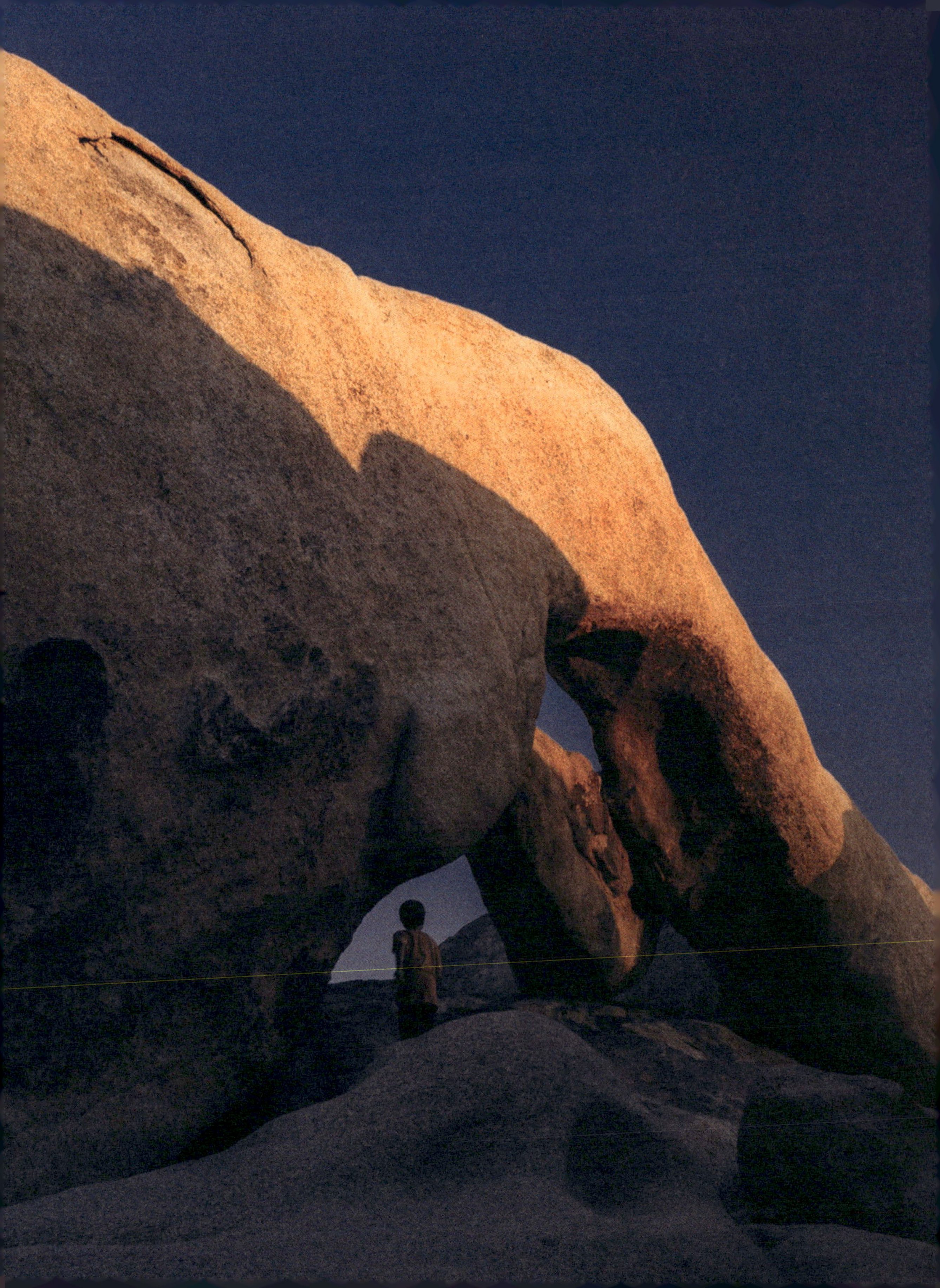

GUIDED PRAYER

1. Meditate on the one thing Jesus says is necessary.

"Martha, Martha, you are anxious and troubled about many things, but one thing is necessary. Mary has chosen the good portion, which will not be taken away from her." Luke 10:41-42

2. Do you feel like you've chosen the good portion, or does your life feel anxious and troubled? Spend time taking an honest look at your life. Allow the Holy Spirit to illuminate what's going on in your heart.

"Casting all your anxieties on him, because he cares for you." 1 Peter 5:7

3. Take time to set boundaries around spending time alone with God. What encroaches on this crucial time? What often takes the place of meeting with God? Why can it be so difficult to fight for time spent at the feet of Jesus? Journal your responses.

In John 15:4 Jesus says, *"Abide in me, and I in you. As the branch cannot bear fruit by itself, unless it abides in the vine, neither can you, unless you abide in me."* In all we do, God desires that we abide in him. We don't leave our time alone with God and then go out into the world without him. He isn't contained to a place or time. His presence is everywhere. Everything we do is an opportunity for relationship with our heavenly Father. He longs to help us do our work effectively with the anointing of the Spirit. He longs to help us love our family and friends. Sitting at the feet of Jesus isn't a time of the day, it's a lifestyle. May you abide in God in all that you do today to his glory and your joy.

Extended Reading: John 15

Vision for Yourself

DAY 24

DEVOTIONAL

For a long time I believed that all God wanted from me was more. I feared he would lead me to more work, more giving, more sacrifice, and less fun. I viewed fun and God as mutually exclusive, as if he was the great cosmic killjoy who only wanted me to sing, fast, pray, and evangelize.

Wrapped up in all my misconceptions was a very me-centric point of view. I thought if I didn't work my fingers to the bone day in and day out for the kingdom that God's will wasn't going to be accomplished. It's as if I believed that I was a savior, the sole hope of the world. And all these misconceptions led to a constant weight I couldn't seem to shake. But Isaiah 55:10-11 says,

For as the rain and the snow come down from heaven and do not return there but water the earth, making it bring forth and sprout, giving seed to the sower and bread to the eater, so shall my word be that goes out from my mouth; it shall not return to me empty, but it shall accomplish that which I purpose, and shall succeed in the thing for which I sent it.

The truth is that God absolutely has good works laid out before me every single day. He has a plan for me that will impact eternity. But his chief desire in everything he asks of me is that we would do it together. He doesn't need me. He wants me. He is not a taskmaster, and I am not his slave. Rather, he calls himself my heavenly Father, and I am to see myself as his son, a coheir with Christ.

> *"I came that they may have life and have it abundantly."*
>
> **JOHN 10:10**

God doesn't desire me to lift a finger if it's not out of love for him. He doesn't need or want any of my works birthed out of a place of striving. He doesn't need or want petty activity, reluctant yeses, programmed words, or burnt-out offerings. Allow the full impact of 1 Corinthians 13:1-3 to hit your heart today. Read it slowly. Allow it to shift your perception of the heart of God:

If I speak in the tongues of men and of angels, but have not love, I am a noisy gong or a clanging cymbal. And if I have prophetic powers, and understand all mysteries and all knowledge, and if I have all faith, so as to remove mountains, but have not love, I am nothing. If I give away all I have, and if I deliver up my body to be burned, but have not love, I gain nothing.

In response to the truth of God's word, we need to have vision for ourselves. We need to set boundaries around our own emotional, physical, and spiritual health. We need to allow God to minister to our weary hearts, shift our perspectives on work, and empower us to live a life marked by inward abundance. What do you need today to enjoy life? What can you do with God rather than for God? What would he use to fill you up to a state of overflowing rather than running on empty?

As you enter into a time of guided prayer, may you find freedom today from the mentality of a slave and live with the joy and peace of a child of the One, True God.

GUIDED PRAYER

1. Meditate on the sovereignty and omnipotence of your heavenly Father. Reflect on his unstoppable ability to accomplish his will.

"For as the rain and the snow come down from heaven and do not return there but water the earth, making it bring forth and sprout, giving seed to the sower and bread to the eater, so shall my word be that goes out from my mouth; it shall not return to me empty, but it shall accomplish that which I purpose, and shall succeed in the thing for which I sent it." Isaiah 55:10-11

2. Meditate on God's desire for love rather than activity.

"If I speak in the tongues of men and of angels, but have not love, I am a noisy gong or a clanging cymbal. And if I have prophetic powers, and understand all mysteries and all knowledge, and if I have all faith, so as to remove mountains, but have not love, I am nothing. If I give away all I have, and if I deliver up my body to be burned, but have not love, I gain nothing." 1 Corinthians 13:1-3

3. What would it look like to live an abundant life today? What do you need to create boundaries around? What would God use today to fill you up and satisfy the dry and weary places in your heart? Take time to rest in the love of God.

"I came that they may have life and have it abundantly." John 10:10

The best boundary for maintaining a sense of health is a having a weekly sabbath. Genesis 2:3 tells us, *"God blessed the seventh day and made it holy, because on it God rested from all his work that he had done in creation."* To rest is holy. It's a declaration to yourself and the world that life is about far more than work. It's a reminder that work is just a way that we live in relationship with God. May you find grace and courage to live in line with the culture of God's kingdom as you set boundaries around what you need in order to live an abundant life.

Extended Reading: Matthew 11

Vision for Others

DAY 25

DEVOTIONAL

One of the greatest joys in life is the gift of serving others. Often in the busyness of work, family, and society we draw boundaries around ourselves so tightly that we don't make room to love others well. God's desire is to shepherd us to a place of inward abundance, not only that we might live in the fullness of life, but also that we would be empowered to give of ourselves to others. Philippians 2:4-8 says,

*"Let each of you look not only to his own
interests, but also to the interests of others."*

PHILIPPIANS 2:4

Let each of you look not only to his own interests, but also to the interests of others. Have this mind among yourselves, which is yours in Christ Jesus, who, though he was in the form of God, did not count equality with God a thing to be grasped, but emptied himself, by taking the form of a servant, being born in the likeness of men. And being found in human form, he humbled himself by becoming obedient to the point of death, even death on a cross.

In his humble, loving sacrifice, Jesus set before us the perfect example of loving others. God might not call all of us to physically die for the sakes of others, but he absolutely leads us to a lifestyle of dying to self that we might live for the kingdom of God. Loving others always requires sacrifice. The gift of love is never free. But in pursuing a lifestyle of looking to the interests of others we'll discover an eternal purpose more fulfilling than any fruit selfishness could produce.

Often, in reading or hearing exhortations centered around serving others, I find myself feeling more and more weighed down. I know that I'm called to love people. I know that I'm called to give of myself. And in response to these emotions I typically engage in a few more activities, find myself empty and burnt out, and subsequently give up on the notion of living sacrificially. But after years of going through this cycle I realized that I was giving, not from a place of love, but out of coercion. I was giving, not as a response to receiving the unconditional love of my heavenly father, but to earn the affection of a Christian community that often admires actions over motives.

But we serve a God who looks at the heart. The call of God on our lives to love others well is designed to flow from a place of fullness and satisfaction. God doesn't ask us to give what we don't have. If you're not in a place of health and abundance, the first step is to ask for the leadership of the Holy Spirit in how he wants to shepherd you to a place of restoration and rejuvenation. The world doesn't need burnt-out givers. God doesn't ask us to die to ourselves if we don't have life to begin with.

God has amazing plans to use you to further his kingdom today. And those plans are filled with acts of love and sacrifice. But before you can love others, you need to know that you are loved. Before you can sacrifice for others, you need to know that Jesus sacrificed for you to a far greater measure than you could ever hope to reciprocate. And in response to God's love and sacrifice, ask him for ways you can love others well. Create boundaries in your life in which you can consistently give of yourself. Seek to look not to your own interests, but to the interests of others.

May you find profound joy and purpose in loving others today in response to God's great love for you.

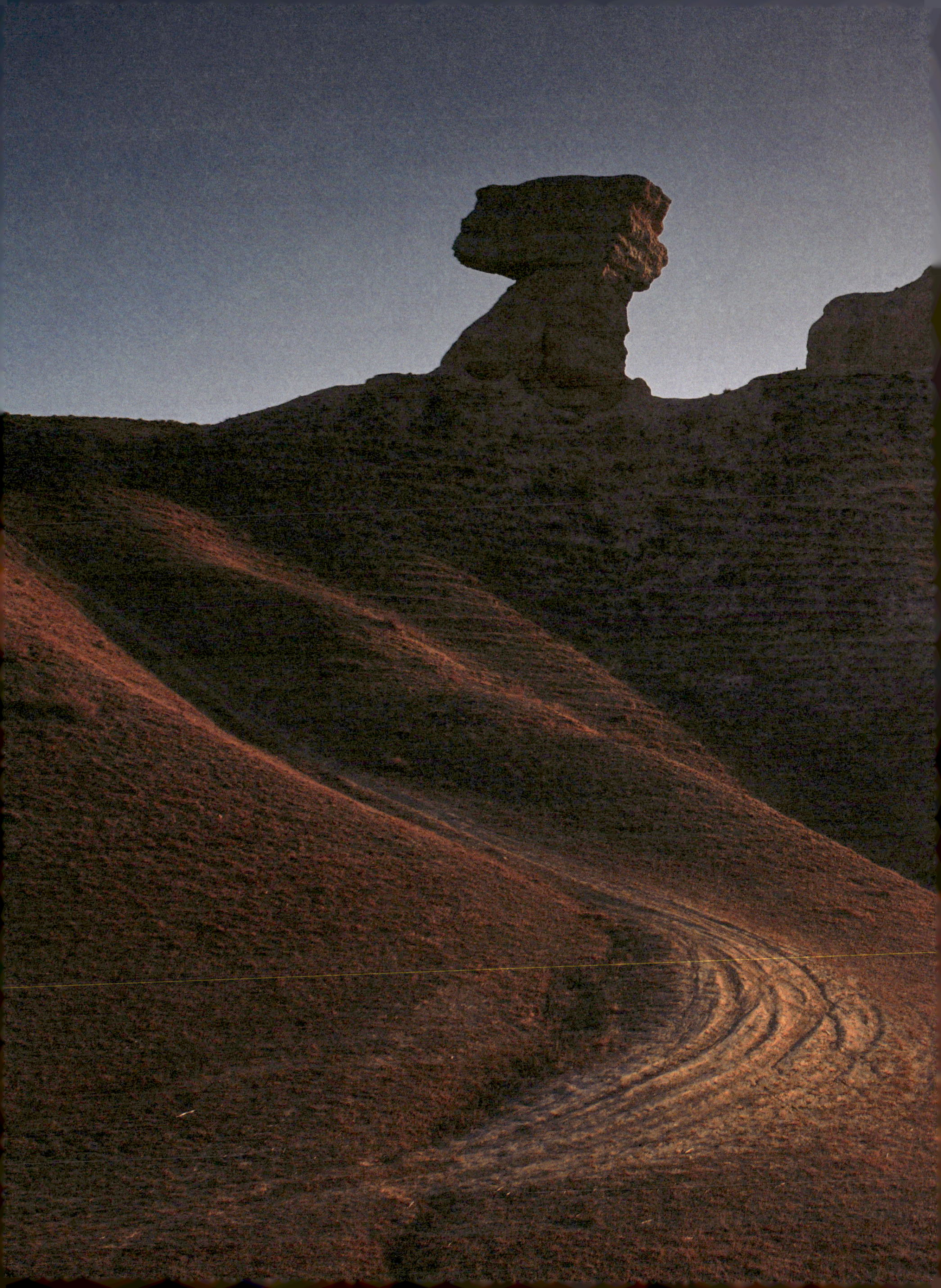

GUIDED PRAYER

1. Meditate on God's unconditional love and overwhelming sacrifice.

"In this the love of God was made manifest among us, that God sent his only Son into the world, so that we might live through him. In this is love, not that we have loved God but that he loved us and sent his Son to be the propitiation for our sins." 1 John 4:9-10

2. Reflect on God's call for you to love and sacrifice for others as a response to his example.

"By this we know love, that he laid down his life for us, and we ought to lay down our lives for the brothers." 1 John 3:16

"Let each of you look not only to his own interests, but also to the interests of others. Have this mind among yourselves, which is yours in Christ Jesus, who, though he was in the form of God, did not count equality with God a thing to be grasped, but emptied himself, by taking the form of a servant, being born in the likeness of men. And being found in human form, he humbled himself by becoming obedient to the point of death, even death on a cross." Philippians 2:4-8

3. In what ways can you love someone well today? Who is God calling you to sacrifice for? In what ways can you give of yourself for the sakes of others? Journal any people or actions who come to mind and commit to the Lord to see them through in his grace.

Inward abundance and rest aren't always necessarily marked by the emotions of happiness or a feeling of energy. Sometimes God asks us to give even when we're weary. Just as Paul walked back into Lystra after being stoned to continue sharing the gospel, we have to get up after being knocked down. Inward abundance is living with an unshakable and unbroken sense of God's love. It's experiencing transcendent joy that can only come from a God whose goodness surpasses the quality of our circumstances. If you will seek to follow the leadership of the Holy Spirit you will know when it's time to rest and time to act. You will know when it's time to retreat with him and time to go out. His leadership will not fail you and his grace will always sustain you. Inquire of the Lord today and discover both restoration and purpose in his steadfast love.

Extended Reading: 1 John 3

Vision for Work

DAY 26

DEVOTIONAL

One of my favorite quotes on work comes from C. S. Lewis, who said, "If God is satisfied with the work, the work may be satisfied with itself." So often I feel unsatisfied in my work. In the age of flexible work hours with never-ending task lists, it's hard to believe that anyone can stop long enough to be satisfied in their work. And in a society where we are what we do, it feels like there is an ever-increasing pressure to work harder, longer, and better. To rest is laziness. To set healthy boundaries is selfish.

But the truth is that the core of boundaries is not selfishness, but stewardship. If we allow our personal lives to get so out of control that they constantly hurt our ability to accomplish the works laid out before us, then we have a problem with stewardship.

And if we don't set healthy boundaries around work to the extent it becomes all-consuming, then we fail to steward ourselves and our ability to love others. We need to get fresh vision for both rest and work. We need to seek a revelation of God's heart for work that our lives would be marked by a sense of satisfaction.

Ephesians 2:10 says, *"For we are his workmanship, created in Christ Jesus for good works, which God prepared beforehand, that we should walk in them."* Have you ever viewed yourself as God's workmanship? Have you ever stopped to think that God designed you with a unique personality, a powerful set of strengths and abilities, and has an eternal purpose for you that you are perfectly designed for? God

> *"Let the favor of the Lord our God be upon us,
> and establish the work of our hands upon us; yes,
> establish the work of our hands!"*
>
> **PSALM 90:17**

doesn't create bad things. He doesn't create without a purpose. Ephesians 2:10 tells us that we are created in Christ Jesus. You are a new creation, filled with the Holy Spirit, and anointed to see God's kingdom come to earth.

If you're lacking vision on what you are to do, look no further than the step in front of you. God has plans for you today that will lead you to tomorrow. He has work for you today that is both valuable in and of itself and will lead you to the next part of his perfect plans. Ecclesiastes 9:10 says, *"Whatever your hand finds to do, do it with your might."* If your desire is to follow God's will, you won't miss it. So often we spend so much time trying to figure out what God wants us to do that we don't do the very work he's laid in front of us. We spend so much time worrying about what we are supposed to accomplish that we never accomplish anything. Absolutely there are times to get vision. Absolutely we are to inquire of the Lord. But rather than asking the Lord for his master plan, enjoy the work he's set before you today. Create boundaries around your work that you might be effective and successful in it and experience the satisfaction of a job well done.

May the prayer of David in Psalm 90:17 be your prayer today as you enter into a time of guided prayer:

"Let the favor of the Lord our God be upon us, and establish the work of our hands upon us; yes, establish the work of our hands!"

WISDOM

GUIDED PRAYER

1. Meditate on your identity as God's workmanship, made new in Jesus.

"For we are his workmanship, created in Christ Jesus for good works, which God prepared beforehand, that we should walk in them." Ephesians 2:10

2. Do you have good boundaries set around your work? Are you valuing the work God's set before you enough? Are you allowing work to seep into every other area of your life? Wherever you are, go to God and ask him how you can better steward your time and energy.

"As each has received a gift, use it to serve one another, as good stewards of God's varied grace." 1 Peter 4:10

3. What work has God set before you to do today? Ask God for the vision and grace to accomplish it well. Take time to find rest and power in his presence.

I pray that as you go about your day today the Lord would reveal your uniqueness to you. I pray that you would find comfort and excitement in the fact that you are fearfully and wonderfully made. I pray that you would find courage in the truth that God has plans and purposes for your life that are unique to you. And I pray you would find power to both work and rest well that you and God might take a look at your day and find satisfaction in it. May your day be filled with the favor of God.

Extended Reading: Romans 12

Vision for Community

DAY 27

DEVOTIONAL

God didn't design you to do life on your own. Scripture is filled with exhortations to engage in community with fellow believers. Galatians 6:2 says, *"Bear one another's burdens, and so fulfill the law of Christ."* Psalm 133:1-3 says, *"Behold, how good and pleasant it is when brothers dwell in unity! . . . For there the Lord has commanded the blessing, life forevermore."* And Ecclesiastes 4:9-12 says,

"Two are better than one, because they have a good reward for their toil. For if they fall, one will lift up his fellow. But woe to him who is alone when he falls and has not another to lift him up! Again,

> *"For where two or three are gathered in my name, there am I among them."*
>
> MATTHEW 18:20

if two lie together, they keep warm, but how can one keep warm alone? And though a man might prevail against one who is alone, two will withstand him—a threefold cord is not quickly broken."

Taking time to invest fully and rightly in community takes both vision and boundaries. Without a sense of God's heart and leadership into fellowship with believers, we'll pull back and isolate when problems arise. And without healthy boundaries around community, we can either allow others to take life from us or not make enough space to give rightly of ourselves.

Take a moment to think about the people God has given you. Think about your friends and family. Think about those around you at church you feel close to. What would life be like if you were all alone? What would your hardships have been like if you absolutely had no one to endure them with? God loves to use others as instruments of his healing. He loves to speak life and restoration into his people through the words and actions of those around them.

But to experience healing, life, and restoration from others is to have the courage to call upon others and be vulnerable. To be in community is to be willing to be the hands and feet of Jesus yourself. It's for that reason that God would have us set healthy, life-giving boundaries for community. If we don't have any margin in our lives to help meet the needs for others, then we've overcommitted ourselves out of a chance to be used by God. And if we don't make time to simply develop friendships and be loved by others, then we miss an opportunity to receive the love and power of God in a real, unique way.

Whether you find yourself overcommitted with community to the level of running on empty, or under-committed to where you feel like you have to do life on your own, there is grace for you today. Today is a new day in which you can make different, life-altering decisions. Today is a day that you can redraw your boundaries and allow God to pour out his Spirit through community.

Take time in guided prayer to receive God's heart for your community. Allow him to fill you with courage to be vulnerable and receive life from others. And ask him to help you draw healthy boundaries that you might give of yourself freely to see others experience life and restoration through the power of God poured out in you.

GUIDED PRAYER

1. Take time to meditate on the importance of community. Allow God to re-envision you for doing life with others.

"Behold, how good and pleasant it is when brothers dwell in unity! . . . For there the Lord has commanded the blessing, life forevermore." Psalm 133:1-3

"Bear one another's burdens, and so fulfill the law of Christ." Galatians 6:2

2. What's going on in your life that needs healing and restoration? In what ways would God use others to bring about that healing and restoration? From whom can you seek wisdom? What friend would God use to fill your life with joy?

"Therefore, confess your sins to one another and pray for one another, that you may be healed. The prayer of a righteous person has great power as it is working." James 5:16

3. Who in your life would God call you to minister to today? Take time to pray for that person and ask God for his heart. Ask him for wisdom and power to love that person well.

"A friend loves at all times, and a brother is born for adversity." Proverbs 17:17

In Acts 2:44-47 we see the power of believers who live in authentic community. Scripture says,

And all who believed were together and had all things in common. And they were selling their possessions and belongings and distributing the proceeds to all, as any had need. And day by day, attending the temple together and breaking bread in their homes, they received their food with glad and generous hearts, praising God and having favor with all the people. And the Lord added to their number day by day those who were being saved.

When God's people gather together and do life in his name, he is there (Matthew 18:20). Seek to develop community that is both fun and representative of the kingdom. Look for others whom you can bring into the community that God's given you. Dwelling in unity with your fellow believers is both a powerful picture of God's heart and a public declaration of his reality and will. May God pour out his Spirit in mighty and powerful ways as you seek to live in God-honoring community.

Extended Reading: Acts 2

Vision for Eternity

DAY 28

DEVOTIONAL

To be a true person of vision is to live this life in light of eternity. Without a real revelation of eternity, this life will be marked by hopelessness and a sense of aimless wandering. Only when our destination comes into view can we rightly see the circumstances strewn along the journey of this life.

"He has made everything beautiful in its time. Also, he has put eternity into man's heart, yet so that he cannot find out what God has done from the beginning to the end."

ECCLESIASTES 3:11

Ecclesiastes 3:11 says, *"He has made everything beautiful in its time. Also, he has put eternity into man's heart, yet so that he cannot find out what God has done from the beginning to the end."* To look to eternity requires us to trust. Our minds are finite. In the only world we've ever known, life is marked by a beginning and end, by birth and death. But in Scripture we discover that God is the Maker of life and the Conquerer of death. We discover that in Jesus we are promised eternal life in unhindered, unveiled communion with our Creator.

To live with vision for eternity is to trust that things are not as they will be and to surrender the entirety of this life with hope for the next. When we live seeking satisfaction from the things of the world, we live as if heaven didn't exist and God didn't usher in his kingdom through Jesus. The things of this world only have value in the Giver of all good gifts. So our possessions, relationships, and work only have value here because they are a shadow of what is to come when all things are made new.

Having vision for eternity should lead us to create boundaries around everything in this life. It should lead us to a lifestyle of surrender that our hearts might never become tied to that which is fleeting and can never fully satisfy. It should lead us to a lifestyle of fully enjoying the things God has given us, all the while knowing the things of this life are merely a shadow in comparison to what is to come.

Do you feel tied to the things of your life today? Do you feel as if your possessions, relationships, and work owns you rather than you enjoying them to the glory of God? Are you seeking to find total satisfaction in the things of the world, or are you finding peace in the hope of heaven? Take time today in guided prayer to surrender your life again to Jesus. Allow God to cut away any ties you have to that which is chaining your heart to this world. And find abundant joy and peace in the freedom that comes from living in light of eternity.

GUIDED PRAYER

1. Meditate on what the Bible says about eternity. Allow Scripture to fill you with vision for what's to come.

"Of old you laid the foundation of the earth, and the heavens are the work of your hands. They will perish, but you will remain; they will all wear out like a garment. You will change them like a robe, and they will pass away, but you are the same, and your years have no end." Psalm 102:25-27

"And this is eternal life, that they know you the only true God, and Jesus Christ whom you have sent." John 17:3

"In my Father's house are many rooms. If it were not so, would I have told you that I go to prepare a place for you? And if I go and prepare a place for you, I will come again and will take you to myself, that where I am you may be also." John 14:2-3

2. Are you living in light of eternity? Do you feel your heart tied down to any things of the world?

"Do not love the world or the things in the world. If anyone loves the world, the love of the Father is not in him." 1 John 2:15

3. Set boundaries around having vision for eternity.
Lay down anything holding you back from living in freedom from this world at the feet of Jesus. Take time to enjoy God that the foundation of your life would be communion with him.

"You make known to me the path of life; in your presence there is fullness of joy; at your right hand are pleasures forevermore." Psalm 16:11

In Galatians 5:16 Paul writes, *"But I say, walk by the Spirit, and you will not gratify the desires of the flesh."* When you take time to enjoy God every day and seek to live in communion with the Holy Spirit, he will faithfully guide you away from the things of the world and into fullness of joy in him. May you find comfort and hope in connection with the living God today as you seek to live with vision for eternity.

Extended Reading: Psalm 102